From The Hospital To The Pulpit

Ronisha Williams

From The Hospital To The Pulpit

Copyright ©2020 Ronisha Williams.

All Rights Reserved.

ISBN:

Published by The Glory Carrier Ministries

No part of this book may be reproduced, stored in a retrieval system or transmitted by any means without written permission from the publisher except for brief quotations in critical reviews or articles.

Unless otherwise noted, Scripture quotations are from the New King James Version and the King James Version. Used by Permission. Scripture quotations marked ASV are from the American Standard Bible Copyright. Scripture quotations marked HCSB are from the Holman Christian Standard Bible. Scripture quotations marked AMP are from The Amplified Bible Copyright © 1954, 1958, 1962, 1964, 1965, 1987 by The Lockman Foundation. All Rights Reserved. Used by Permission

From The Hospital To The Pulpit

From The Hospital To The Pulpit

Dedication

To my amazing Husband of 20 years, Arthur Williams: Thank you for loving me through it all. You are the epiphany of a man who truly loves Christ and his wife. You helped me come from bondage to liberty in God. You saw in me a mighty woman of God, you brought out the BEST in me. I love you.

Thank you to my mother, Alice Henderson who I love and adore. You are a true jewel in my life. I love you more than you will ever know. Your destiny is great and I will forever fight for it.

And to my children, you are three beautiful blessings. You all are one of the reasons I kept fighting, I kept pushing.

To my amazing JUUT family, I love you all you will always be my family.

To my phenomenal BFF Latisha White and goddaughter thank you for your unconditional love towards me. Thank you for seeing the God in me and never giving up on me. Love you both so very much.

From The Hospital To The Pulpit

Table of Contents

Dedication: 4

Introduction: 7

Chapter One: Blink Of An Eye 10

Chapter Two: Entrapped With Emotions 22

Chapter Three: Deep Wounds 31

Chapter Four: The Heart of Resentment 39

Chapter Five: A Grasp On Life 45

Chapter Six: The Question Of Why 55

Chapter Seven: The Critical Hour 61

Chapter Eight: The Journey 81

Chapter Nine: Breakthrough At The Door 104

The Introduction

I will bless the Lord at all times. His praise shall continually be in my mouth. Psalms 34:1.

I will forever be thankful unto God for bringing me over every mountain. God brought me from a survivor to an overcomer there is definitely a huge difference.

Galatians 5:1 says, "Stand fast therefore in the liberty wherewith Christ hath made us free and be not entangled again with the yoke of bondage."

This scripture is a testament of what God did and what I will never return too. I still wake up and pinch myself because it all seems so unreal. I'm actually free. No longer pretending the love is real, my smile is real and I know my God is definitely real. Where would I be without the mercy and grace of God? He has kept me. After reading this book, I guarantee your life will never be the same.

From The Hospital To The Pulpit

I'm a living, breathing, walking miracle that God can and still heals. I'm living proof of the reality of Jesus He is a mighty deliverer. As you journey through my story, be open, honest and let God flow the way He wants. Don't hold back, because you're next in line for your miracle. To my loving sister, my only sister LaSaundra Dagenais, today is your day too. You have been my support system over the years. I love and appreciate you so much. As you begin to read, ask the Lord to have His way and penetrate and touch every area of your life. God sees you when no one does and it's your time. I look forward to hearing all the amazing testimonies. Thank you for your love and support of me and my journey to wholeness. Remember God is not a respecter of persons. If He did it for me, He will do it for you.

From The Hospital To The Pulpit

Chapter One

Blink of an Eye

It all happened so fast. It was within a blink of an eye I went from being healthy, well, living out my dreams to fighting for my life. I thought I had it going on. I just finished school a few months prior and got hired at my dream job. Everything seemed so perfect. I was doing what I loved to do, hair. I loved making people look and feel good about themselves. When I was in beauty school, I struggled so hard to finish. Through it all, I continued to press because my heart was in it and my mind was made up to finish. For six months, I went to school for six days straight, eight hours every day. Through all the drama and minor setbacks, I finished with an A. I received a 95.6%, I finally did it. Prior to graduating, I got hired at my dream job, Juut. When I was younger, I used to say whenever I would ride by there and see it on Grand that was my job. I was going to work there someday. My hopes and dreams were high and I was set on that job. I finally got it. I had a job before graduating and I was proud of myself. After graduating, I had a month and a half before I started working. A lot had taken place, during this time. I relocated to a new church that was starting from the ground up with about eight members. A lot of new, exciting things was happening for me and I was enjoying every moment of it. I spent the summer with the kids until it was time to start my new career.

My first day of work had come and I was excited. I got up, got dressed and headed to work. Upon arrival, I was there with three other people I went to school with. It was comforting knowing some people at work. The first two weeks at work was learning all about Juut and what to expect. I learned one thing that set us apart from other salons and that was we were Day Makers. I loved that and the meaning behind being a Day Maker. After two weeks at work, I took my first guest after that I soared at my job. I enjoyed every moment of being there and being a part of this amazing team. It wasn't just a job; it was my second home. We were all like family. It didn't seem like I had a care in the world. I had my job, a new church, the same people from my old church, but it felt like a fresh start. I was working, going to church and enjoying life. I never once thought things would change but only get better. Four months had passed by and I was three weeks shy of entering into element 3 of training at my job. Things were about to changed in what seemed to be a blink of an eye. The end of

From The Hospital To The Pulpit

the year had approached and I was excited to begin a new chapter in my life. It was December 31st, 2012. I had attended watch night service at our former church. It was a great service and we brought in the New Year right.

The morning of Jan. 4th, 2013, I got up as I did every morning for work. However this morning for some odd reason felt different. My chest was bothering me but I continued to press I went to work anyway. Upon arrival to work my first guest was my boss. I had to do a blowout. I remember I began to struggle doing her hair. My chest tightened more and more. I could feel the pressure. When I was done, I couldn't take my next guest, I was weak. I struggled to get to one of my boss offices. When I got there, I slipped into the chair as they called 911. When the ambulance arrived, they hooked me up to a machine gave me a shot in the arm and rushed me to Methodist Hospital. When I got to the hospital, I was intubated for the very first time in my life and placed in ICU. They said I had the flu, it was bad. This was the year the flu was very bad and people were losing their life from it. A lady next door to me passed away from the flu, while I was fighting for my life in my room. I stayed on the breathing machine for 4 days. On the fourth day I pulled the tubes out my mouth. They kept them out because my breathing stabilized. The next day, I was transferred out of ICU and placed on another floor. In those four days, I lost 14lbs and still was very weak but was improving or so I thought. When the doctors came in, they noticed I could not stand without collapsing. They begin to get concerned and sent me to the operating room for a spinal tap. Upon returning to my room, within hours I could no longer feel my legs. The doctors told me I had a disease called GBS (Guillain-Barre Syndrome). It's a disease where your immune system attacks the nerve system in your body. It cause paralysis throughout your body. The doctors came back and rushed me back to the operating room to place a catheter in my chest. The catheter ran from just above my collar bone to the major vein in my heart. I had to go through 5 treatments of plasma apheresis to cleanse my blood. By the time my second treatment hit, I lost all my ability to move my legs and right side of my body.

I stayed in the hospital for three weeks and then was transferred to rehab. Going through this at first never moved me because I thought it would be over soon. I thought that it was temporal. When I arrived to rehab reality set in. I had to go through intense physical therapy 3 hours a day. The first week I was put on a dysphagia diet because I could not swallow. Reality set in and I was scared for the very first time in my life. I didn't talk the same. I couldn't do anything on my own everything was done for me. When the days were over and the lights were out and it was just me and God. I cried and cried; I really did. I felt alone and heartbroken. Within hours my life changed and within weeks it seemed hopeless. I stayed in rehab for a month and it was the most trying time of my life. I went from being totally independent to completely dependent on people taking care of me, helping me. I was away from my family and it was tough. You think in life you know who is for you and who has your back, but when you're faced with life trials you find out who is really for you. I can count on my hand the number of visitors I had. Everyone who I thought was in my life and cared never came by, never visited or called. Some did at the very end it hurt deeply. Being in rehab was so challenging for me. Those that came had their opinion as to why I got sick and why I was going through this storm. Truth be told God had His hand in it from the beginning. My husband and kids spent countless hours with me in rehab. A former Pastor and his wife came by and so did one of my mentors from CTAC. A week into doing rehab I was rushed back to the hospital to the cardiac floor. My heart rate was high and also my blood pressure. I went through extensive tests for my heart.

It was scary my heart was in distress. I stayed in the cardiac unit for a week until I got better and was ready to return to rehab. I returned to rehab to continue my recovery. I spent two more weeks in rehab and then was able to go home. Before going home, I had all my care set up and went home with a walker and wheelchair. I had physical therapy and occupational therapy set up to continue at home. Adjusting to being home was not an easy transition because I was not the same. My physical condition was not the same. It was so hard and heartbreaking. I was so used to getting up doing everything on my own. Now, I was dependent upon my loved ones to help care for me. Only a few was there. My husband struggled to make sure I had what I needed and worked. Thank God for my job because they really helped out. They sent food to my house every week for my family. They also sent large donations to help us out financially. They were a huge blessing because we needed help. My former pastor and his wife helped out financially with what they could, they were a blessing as well. They gave support through love, prayer and visiting that was comforting for me. It just felt like a very lonely place, when you think people love you and care and in the moment of a crisis you find out who is really there. While I was home, within a week I was rushed back to the hospital and intubated again. I stayed in the hospital for 3 weeks. During this time my job visited me and updated everyone I worked with. Though I didn't see them much physically, you felt the outpouring love and support from them. It was a blessing and it helped me in

From The Hospital To The Pulpit

the most difficult time in my life. After three weeks in the hospital, I went home and was there for about 2 weeks and was back in the hospital again intubated for the third time. I only stayed a week and was sent back home to continue home therapy. I regained my feeling in my legs and upper body. I was still pretty weak and because of the disease it caused my breathing muscles to become very weak. For the next two months, I was rushed back to the hospital intubated every time. Then in April, I was not feeling well and I went to the hospital not knowing it would be another change to my life within a blink of an eye. I was admitted to the University of Minnesota and there begin to go through extensive testing. I spent a week in the hospital. My mom was at the hospital visiting me when the doctor told me if I could walk to the end of the hall I could go home. Upon walking by the time I got mid-way through with the nurse on my side, I collapsed I don't remember much. They said I flat lined and the doctors rushed to my aide. I was stabilized minutes later and in the critical care unit. When I came to the doctors said you won't be going home. They said they needed to run more tests and figure out what was going on with me. I was very weak and needed answers to what was going on with me. My lungs were moving with very little air and my ABG blood gas was low every time they took it. I was sent down to see a lung specialist a few days later which determined I had severe asthma. They started me on asthma medications that day and steroids. I started four meds that day. I was also put on oxygen and scheduled to do a test for my breathing. I was also scheduled for a six-minute walk test. The walk test was scheduled first but it was determined to dangerous to send my body through because every time I would attempt to walk my oxygen levels would drop very low quickly. Sometimes, it would be so severe while trying to walk I would pass out. So, I couldn't perform the walk test. Then the oximetry test came and I had to be off of all machines. But that didn't last long. My oxygen levels dropped and after taking another blood gas test, it matched my oxygen levels. The doctors determined I needed a BiPAP machine every night and continuous oxygen. I also couldn't stand or walk without oxygen when they would try and walk me, I could not walk very far. I spent the next 5 weeks in the hospital. It was hard being there and trying to adapt to these changes. It was rough being away from my family not seeing my kid's every day, waking up to them and seeing them off to school. The things in life we take for granted I now struggle to have. Taking showers was eliminated from my daily schedule it was too risky and dangerous for my breathing. My husband would come every day and some days bring the kids. I began rehab at the hospital mainly trying to build endurance for my body so I could begin to

From The Hospital To The Pulpit

walk without complications. I also went through a range of tests at the University of Minnesota. My body was changing and things could be very critical at times. Along with my oxygen, I now had to be very careful with my heart rate and blood pressure POTS disease is what they called it. The list of medical problems was increasing. Imagine going through it and experiencing it in your body. It was a nightmare. So moving along, I spent 6 weeks in the hospital. My birthday and mother's day was spent in the hospital. I was so ill it was affecting every core of my being both mentally and spiritually. I went home in May on home oxygen and a BiPAP machine and a host of other medical equipment. My life once again had a medical change that altered my life in a great way. My life revolved around a green cylinder tank filled with oxygen and a clear cannula that wrapped around my face and hung around my ears. I couldn't breathe without it. If I traveled outside the home, I had to take a few tanks with me. It was such a hassle at times. It annoyed me when I would go out and people would just stare me down. They looked as if they never saw anyone with oxygen on, boy did that bother me. I was beginning to feel the effects of being sick mentally depression sank deep within. The feeling of hopelessness was all so real. Being surrounded by people that had their opinions about me and why I was sick did not help the matter at all. I did not really want to hear anyone's opinion at all. In fact that was all it was. I felt a huge feeling of resentment come over me for some of them. One person came to my house and told me I was sick because I needed to get it together for my kids or they wouldn't make it. That drew a line with me and that person. I didn't want to see them coming. It made my bones cringe inside, like how dare you. I knew inside they didn't have a clue to what I was going through or what I was feeling inside. The mere fact that they had the audacity to even come to my house at such a difficult time and say a bunch of nothing to me then end with I love you was crazy. Over the years, everything that I thought was felt about me was true and it manifested during this time. I had so many feelings going on the inside and if you blew on me, I would have falling right over the edge. My life had changed. It changed dramatically and I was feeling the effects of it. I mean going through this people really showed their true colors. One family member told me they prayed that the disease would kill me. Really? I was going to overcome this. It was only a matter of time. I was hurting inside and out physically and spiritually sick in a dark hole that only God could bring me out of. I was taking over 19 medications a day some of them pain medication. Some of my days would be filled with drowsiness.

From The Hospital To The Pulpit

I continued to get stronger at home seeing the home care team, doing physical therapy and occupational therapy at home. Most of my days were a blur, due to all the medication I was on.

The summer was here and I wanted to enjoy it the best way I could. I started to go back to church coming and being there seemed like a big blur. I existed in a huge room physically but mentally and spiritually I was far gone from that place I once called my home. I was disconnected from it; my body was there but not my mind and heart.

The emotional wounds were open, and all I could see was that I was alone, hurting, desperate to be healed but wasn't. I seemed to be greeted with smiles and hugs some of whom I could have cared less. After all they said words that cut the core of me and was very insensitive toward my situation. I do understand now that they were loving and giving me only what they knew. It was just heartbreaking because I needed God not opinions.

I said to myself, "Lord, help me that when I come out of this, I am sensitive to you first and that I may be sensitive to others around me and their needs." I asked God to help me not to render my opinion but to speak only that which He had given me to say. Ephesians 4:29 says, "Let no corrupt communication proceed out of your mouth, but that which is good to the use of edifying, that it may render grace to the hearers." I needed to be edified not trampled on and kicked while I was already down. One thing my former mentor did was nature wounds that needed to be healed. She didn't give up on me and she understood where I was. She cried with me prayed with me and for that I am always grateful even in her absence now in my life. She was a beacon of light in my life and she still is to this day one of my hero's. She spoke life when others were not, she believed in the call upon my life. She pushed, poured and prayed from the place she was in God. My BFF was there too, she never left my side she would travel from Wisconsin just to be with me. I had love around me but because of what I was dealing with I still felt empty on the inside. That's a deep place to be in only God and bring me out to complete healing in Him.

Chapter Two

Entrapped With Emotions

Some days, I would sit in my room and just cry as I wondered why. How could everything I dreamed of and worked so hard for be ripped right from under me? This seemed so unbearable and at times like it was crushing the very core of my being. Not only was I suffering but so were my children and husband. They were hurting and it was beginning to show. When I was away for long periods of time at the hospital they suffered. They did not have anyone to be there spiritually, emotionally or hardly physically. My husband was trying all he could to work and to pay the bills. The kids spent countless hours at home alone until he got home. My daughter who was so attached to me was suffering badly. Her hair had falling out because it was not being taken care of when I was away and that bothered me. My husband was hurting and some days he would just cry. He was so broken because he could not help me. For the first time in our marriage he felt helpless. My family including me was broken we felt alone a lot of times as if no one was there at all. I know someone reading this feels like this right now but hold on because the word of God says Joshua 1:9, "Have not I commanded thee? Be strong and of a good courage; be not afraid, neither be thou dismayed: for the Lord thy God is with thee whithersoever thou goest."

Back to my story, I was the trend setter in my home, and when I got sick, it affected everything and everyone. My husband had to do everything I was doing on top of try and work to pay bills and maintain his own sanity. With me being home, the kids were better because they could see me every day and be around me, touch me, and hug me. For me, it was an emotional meltdown and I was about to crack at any given moment. I finally got my mother to come over. She spent the week at my house and cooked and cleaned. She was trying to fatten me up because I was frail and thin and she did just that. That weekend my family had come up here from out of state and came over my house seeing me like that I guess they couldn't understand because they laughed and laughed at me. They laughed at the way I walked, talked and moved about it was not funny to me it crushed me. I couldn't wait until they left so I could get some peace and quiet time to regroup.

From The Hospital To The Pulpit

Depression seemed at any given moment to take over it was only a matter of time. I thought over and over about my life and where it was. This can't be real; no this is not true. It's a dream and I'm going to wake up soon. Pinch, pinch I'm not awake yet; pinch, pinch still not awake. This was reality. This was real and no waking up to what already was. As I drowned in depression and medications, it kept my mind in a blah moment and I didn't have to deal with the reality of my life. When I would be home, I would just sleep and sleep hardly move from one spot to another. I spent most of my time in my room on my bed. The pastor of my now former church would come at times to visit or just sit and watch me as he studied the word of God until the kids got home. Some days, I was able to go to church sit and hear the worship and word of God. When it was over, I was still broken, still hurt, still depressed and still messed up not because they weren't able to help me. They just could not help me. This thing I was going through was between me and God and He let me know that on the hospital bed in rehab. Being home at times, I would sit in my room and depression would consume me to the point I wanted to die. That was the first stage of me starting to cut myself. One cut landed me in the hospital with 39 stitches. They admitted me because of my medical history and condition over the past year. I stayed 8 days and was discharged home adding two new medications to my med list. One was a blood thinner with shots I had to take twice a day. So now, I'm taking 21 medications on top now having to stick myself daily with a needle. Were these people crazy? They want me to die right? No they didn't they were saving my life. I get home hardly wanting to look at those shots but I had to take them. Although I landed me in the hospital, God had me and it saved my life. The home health nurse came to check my wound every other day and to make sure I was taking my meds properly. My baby girl helped me out a lot she wanted to be a doctor and she was very educated on my care. She would listen at the hospital visits and when the nurses would come to the house or whenever the ambulance had to be called, she knew exactly what to do what to say. She was my life saver, my little angel sent from above. She was so sensitive to my needs and my condition. Even though I was on an emotional roller coaster and depression was overwhelming my life, I did not have the strength to take my life because of my kids. I loved them too much. I thought they deserved better than what was handed to them and I needed to at least try and fight through this. When your back is against the wall, and everything is falling all around you, please grab hold of God through faith. With the last ounce you have within fight and never give up. You have to touch the Holy Ghost. Touch means to cling onto. You have to in your darkest hour cling onto

Him until your change comes. Don't let go! You're coming out too. My kids deserved the best in life. My husband needed me also so with all that in mind I didn't take my life at all. I was emotionally wrecked but not destroyed. My pain was birthing my destiny and purpose. Let that pain birth power and don't give in like I did but push through it. I cried so many tears. Sometimes, crying so hard my body jerked I just wanted this all to be over. I wanted my life back and it all seemed impossible. It felt like I fought hard to get to where I was just to have it all taken away from me. I was an emotional wreck. My emotions were all over the place and I went from 0 to 10 in a matter of seconds. Some of the hurt I was feeling was turning bitter and I could feel the rage whaling inside me. Every emotion you can think of I had and was dealing with. It had my mind racing a million miles an hour. The hurt and wounded little girl inside me was beginning to surface. I did not want to deal with her at all. I am usually able to bury her deep down inside so she does not interrupt my adult life. What I was going through was pushing hard on me and she was beginning to surface and it seemed like I had no control over her.

How It All Started

When you take a glance at my life you would think oh, she so pretty, she have a beautiful family, a car and a nice house. You would think I had it all together pretty well put you could say. Whatever I wanted I got and if I didn't have it well let's just say I made myself have it. I looked pretty good on the outside looking in and before this storm hit my home, I thought I was all that and some. You couldn't tell me anything. I had a very high-end apartment. $1600 was the rent per month. I had a brand new 2012 car. I mean I was living it up. I was living the life I always dreamed of having. My kids were good, husband was good and life to me as you know it was golden. Went to church faithfully and sang on the praise team. I mean this was the life for me. You know that was my way of a good life but God had different plans in mind for me. Although I was looking good on the outside and had everything I wanted or ever needed, I was messed up on the inside. If you truly saw past the surface of my looks and what I had you could see a wounded little girl who felt abused, misused, abandoned, rejected, sad, hurt and very angry. I had buried these things over the years. I didn't want anyone to know about this little girl living on the inside of me. I wanted to keep her hidden keep the secrets hidden. When I was a child I vowed before I turned 18 that I would never let anyone hurt me again and that I would live a life that I felt was good for me. The walls were built up so you could not get that close to me. I learned to mask every wound I had from childhood to my adult life.

From The Hospital To The Pulpit

When I turned 18 years, family was banking on me turning into a stripper or prostitute. I had a different outcome in my mind and so did the Lord. I knew I was an emotional wreck and when I became a young adult, I was determined to bury that part of me. I gave my life to the Lord at the age of 18 doing that was the best decision I ever made. That was June of 1999 church was new for me. I was not raised in church and had no church background and I was sure about to pay for that soon. I started going to church regularly with my sister and aunt. We all gave our lives to Christ around the same time. I met some new people my husband being one. He got my number a few weeks after I got saved. We talked often and hung out. He would call and pray with me and talk to me about the word. This was something I was not use to so at times I would be very mean. Then my heart started shifting toward him. I can't explain it but it did. By October, we were dating a few was against it. This was another blow to my already wounded spirit. People thought he was too good for me. I was not good enough for him. People at church start talking to me and telling me not to date him. Others just let me know they did not support us dating with their actions. I didn't understand and it was hurt packing on to a little girl that was not healed yet. By December, Arthur proposed to me in front of his family and mine. I said yes. So not only was I only 18 newly saved but, I was about to be married soon at a young age. Now with us getting engaged it made some matters worse at church we did not have much support at all. It didn't matter what anyone thought and said. We were in love and wanted to spend the rest of our lives together. For the next few months, we spent nearly every day together he introduced me to things I never had, places I've never gone and things I never did. We did so much together. I didn't have time to deal with the hurting little girl inside me. I was busy with church and Arthur. Tuesdays, Thursdays and Saturdays and Sunday's I was in the church building. I was excited about being saved and I was on fire for the Lord. My zeal for Him was intense.

Arthur and I didn't set a date yet for getting married that was quickly about to change. Arthur was so in love with me that he could hardly stay focused. He start being late to work and he would call me all the time. On February 1st, 2000, I moved into my own place with Arthur's help. I got a 2-bedroom apartment on the Eastside of Saint Paul. My mother gave me her furniture set she brought a few months prior to me moving. I had a television and brought my bed from my mother's house. Arthur and I still were not married yet and because we spent so much time together, we end up sleeping together before we were married. The next month in March one of our former pastor called us told us the Lord dealt with him and told him to marry us.

We went got our marriage license and on Thursday, March 30th, 2000, we got married right after Bible study. I was 18 years old he was 22 at the time of our marriage. Our former pastor blessed us and sent us on our way. Arthur moved all his things into my apartment after we got married. The night we got married we didn't have a honeymoon at all I had decided to babysit my cousin. I was young and didn't know any better. I didn't know how to be a wife neither did I have an example of it. The night of our marriage I felt the wounded little girl arise in me she had been dormant for years. It was crazy because before we got married all I wanted was him and to be around him but when we got married things didn't seem the same. I was an emotional wreck and I managed to bury that hurt and build strong walls around me that didn't seem to be working.

Chapter Three

Deep Wounds

I am 18 married and just found out that I am pregnant with my first child. My husband lost his job because he couldn't get to work and I was not working at all. So how are we going to pay these bills? Living on my own was new for me and quite new for my husband as well. We got help with our rent from our church, so that saved us from being put out for a month. June was here I got a job in Saint Paul at a daycare center. It wasn't in time to pay for our rent we were late on so we had to move. I was 3 months pregnant and had to move back in with my mom. It was so embarrassing for me. My mom let Arthur stay there with me. I went to work every day on time. I walked from University and Hamlin to Grand and Lexington abcut 2 miles to work and 2 miles back. Arthur still was not working so we couldn't afford another apartment with just my income. We moved back and forth from my mother's to his and things were always uneasy for both of us. I always felt out of place at his mother house and he didn't like to be at my mother's because of the environment. The stress was piling on we argued almost every day. This was a storm like no other everything we were going through was so hard. People at church made fun of us. They cracked jokes about our marriage and circumstances around it. They made bets as to how long we would stay married family did too. This was a disaster, and I wished it all would just go away.

August arrived I got up for work, as usual, I was five months pregnant I got dressed, as always Arthur walked me all the way to work. My stomach was cramping on the way, but it was not cramping that had me concerned. When I got to work mid-way through the day, I started experiencing deep pain in my stomach. This pain was so bad I balled up in a ball at work and cried as they called 911. I was rushed to Regions hospital, where they admitted me saying the baby and I were in danger and I needed to give birth. My family came to the hospital as well my former pastor and a few ministers at the church. I told the doctor I was not having my baby even if it meant my life. I wanted my baby, and I was not going out without a fight. The doctors said I needed to give birth and that my baby would have a 2% chance of surviving after being born. I was not letting up. I was going to continue to carry my baby to term even if it meant my life. I had an infection in my amniotic fluid. The pastor, ministers and my husband prayed over my unborn child and me. When the doctors came back, we had them redo the test, and they came back inconclusive. God touched my body through prayer. I was thankful and at peace with everything. I was put on bedrest stayed in the hospital for eight days and went home on meds. I was on a medication that kept me from having contractions it helped the baby to carry to term. So much was going on in my life and with no place to stay, I was considered a high-risk pregnancy. On top of that, I didn't have my job anymore. It was ok because my husband finally found a job it wasn't too far from my mother's house. We didn't have a car. We still went back and forth with our parents and it was tough I hated every moment of it. Bedrest was hard to be on because I could not sit still. I went into preterm labor a few times and was admitted to the hospital to keep contractions under control. I was having a boy and he was due December 15th, 2000. In November, Arthur's mother threw me a baby shower at the church. I got everything I needed and some. My mom also threw me a baby shower, and it turned out nice. I was so excited to be having a baby boy. We had his name before he was born. God gave us the name Adriel which mean God is our help. That name was so fitting being that God helped me through a very harsh and critical pregnancy. Adriel came seven days past his due date on December 22, 2000, weighing 7lbs 11oz. I went into labor at 1 am that morning. It was a Friday I had done communion at church the night before. I felt fine. I got up went into the hospital my contractions were eight minutes apart. When I got settled in my room, they checked me told me I was 3 centimeters dilated and they were keeping me. I was put in another room told to try and rest. It was going to be a long night. In my room, I laid down and rested the contractions still were eight minutes apart. I fell asleep waking up every now and then if the contractions were rough. I woke up the next morning with an urge to push they checked me and behold; I was 10 centimeters dilated. They broke my water bag. Doing so a piece of skin got caught on the baby. I pushed from 9 am that morning until 1:19 pm when Adriel was born weighing 7lbs 11oz. I beat the odds to God be the glory. My baby was healthy and big. He was my miracle son. I was so happy to see him. My room was filled with family and Adriel's God mom. After meeting him, I got cleaned up and hugged my baby and held him. He was someone to love of my own. I had him December 22nd at 1:19 pm. I went home Christmas Eve morning back to my mother's house. I took my baby upstairs where I was staying and laid down. I was sore and tired motherhood had kicked in fast. My husband was a proud father and happy to meet his first son.

On Christmas, we went over to my in-law's house stayed for a little while. Not all day because I was so sore and achy all over. Now we had a baby living with my parents and dealing with the ups and downs of marriage and some folk at church who just talked a bunch of garbage about us. Not everyone talked a few prayed for us and encouraged us. Others talked and gossiped about us, but that didn't keep us from going to church. I have to mention we were sat down at church because we had sex before marriage, they thought I was pregnant before I was actually pregnant. I thought I was too but I wasn't. Going through all this church stuff was new to me, but they treated me like I was aware of all these church rules and regulations. Going through this was horrible everyone had their opinions about me, my marriage and my baby. I was 19 years old a year shy of being saved, a wife and a mother.

The little girl in me hasn't surfaced to the degree yet, but after all these blows from so many people she was bound to surface real soon. Wound after wound, I wondered what was wrong with these people they had no compassion, no nothing just pure harshness. After seven months of staying with my parents, and in-laws we got an apartment just 5 minutes from my mother. It was a two bedroom, very nice and to show you how good God is our whole apartment was furnished for us. We had everything. We had a living room set, bed sets, kitchen set and tons of household items. Our first apartment together as a family was nice. It felt good to be in our own home. It was so peaceful, but that was not going to last long. The little wounded little girl inside me was about to surface in an ugly way. Arthur and I haven't had any real enjoyment being married we were going through from the start of our marriage. Living with my now husband was different and I was not used to it I screamed every chance I got. We argued almost every day. To make matters worse both sides of the family inserted themselves into our marriage. My family was not saved and very unchurched, but his was. I was blamed for talking to folk I thought I trusted in the church that spread our business. There seemed to be no real outlet. Everywhere I turned was just a mess and a mouth full of opinions void of God's word. I was emotionally unstable. My soul was restless and it showed in my actions. If I didn't like you, it would show. If you hurt me, oh boy would I let you know with my body language. I didn't even understand my own self at times. I felt the hurt and pain was real. I was wounded deeply not knowing how to check my emotions I was an emotional wreck. I found myself getting upset over the smallest things and I was moved by everyone's opinion of me. So many nights I was up crying about what someone else said about me. My self-esteem was shattered. I will discussed that in my next chapter. My attitude shifted daily it was always up and down happy then sad and cold them warm what was wrong me? I know I was wounded deeply I needed God but didn't know how to reach Him, I mean truly reach Him. I was so deeply wounded I tried to live according to the way people wanted me to according to the way they thought my life should be. I can still hear the words ring in my ear, "Ronisha, if you do this and this your marriage will be better. Or if you do this list of things your husband will be this." It was always evolved around my husband because according to some I was surrounded with, I was the hindrance in our lives. I was holding him up in ministry and he was stagnant because of me. Yeah, all these years of false lies and a falsified truth. I was so wounded I thought my life was too hopeless to try and fix, put back together again. The same people that said all these things used that same voice to say I was going to be great in God. Confused? Yes, I was. I just never understood that method of life and it always baffled me. I tried all the things they would tell me, but it still left me empty, hurt, and broken. I cried puddles of tears. I did desire to be right before God but man what chance did I really have in this life with who I was around. They judged the shell I hid myself in and what they thought but failed to see me as God did. They couldn't discern the deep-rooted hurt girl.

From The Hospital To The Pulpit

If I felt, you thought some type of way about me I would act the way I thought you were thinking of me. 9 out of 10 times I was right because it would eventually come out. When we would have family gatherings and it came to me everyone would tell me I had come a long way. Sometimes pointing out things I did. Of course, it would be centered on my husband. I started to get tired of hearing the same old stuff, and eventually resentment festered in my heart. Those deep wounds had now drawn out to be bitterly cold and resentful.

Chapter Four
Resentment At Its Best

It's a dangerous place to be in when you allow resentment to settle in your heart. I had my second son by this time and we had moved into a 3-bedroom house in a very nice neighborhood. I started putting more time into my appearance than working on what was on the inside of my heart. I was bitter, angry and hurt and my attitude of not caring showed. I went to church every week put on my best fit, though I looked good on the outside but I was one bitter, angry lady. I got into with a few people. If you said something we would argue and some of us just wouldn't speak for sometime. I did not care one bit. I was angry mad at the world and if you did not speak to me, I didn't speak to you. This was very petty and it took two to tangle. Some of the people that called themselves spiritual would try and be what they called real with me and tell it like it was. It only penetrated a deep wound that was already there. The love some had for me was based on how I was with my husband or how I treated him or how I was with my children. It is crazy but true. And, the sad part is I wanted to be accepted by them and for them to think the world of me. That would soon change though. I was assigned a mentor that would forever alter and change the course of my life for good. She came into my life at a critical point. I was messed up, bitter, unforgiving and angry. Yes, that was me. I was hanging on by a thread. She came into my life and said I am with you every step of the way. She hugged me and cried with me on the bathroom floor at church. Finally, someone truly had my back and saw me for me not for who they wanted me to be. She saw past the surface and saw the hurting little girl inside that was wounded to the very core of her soul. God knew what I needed and when I needed it. He was sure to come to my rescue real soon.

I went to a sisterhood retreat, we did this activity, and that was the first door I had walked through that would change things in me. We had to create a poem of our life read it. When I stood up to read mines I broke down and started crying. I was shocked. Why couldn't I control these tears? And, oh the pain I was feeling was awful. I could hardly make it through reading the poem. My chest was tightening up the pressure was so intense. Ok, I was almost at the end. I saw the light. I thought keep reading, keep reading you're almost done. With every breath I took, it felt like eternity. Whew, then finally a sigh of relief I made it to the end and I was still standing. I sat in my chair and thought where did all that come from? I wasn't expecting it and neither did I plan what was happening to me that night. I went home and went to bed. Upon waking up that morning, my chest felt like it was caving in. My husband didn't know what to do. He called for prayer and then called 911. The ambulance arrived because my chest was hurting, they moved quickly and brought me into the hospital. They checked me over only to discovered that I had a very bad panic attack. Later that night when I got home, I had two voicemails from two members of our church. They were crying and praying in tongues on my voicemail telling me they knew what I was going through and to give them a call. I didn't call, but I listened to the voicemail and continued on my day. I know after that weekend something changed, and it was whaling up inside me, and I didn't like what I was feeling. Was the little girl finally being exposed? What was going on with me? I still felt resentment, bitterness, rage and the list goes on. It seemed to be bubbling up all at once and oh my, this was not good for me. I thought about what was going on in my life, over the years the root of bitterness was strongly rooted in my heart. It blindsided me for a while and for the first few years of salvation the more I suppressed it, the stronger it became. If you mentioned a name, I would almost cringe in my bones, and it was not a good feeling. Once bitterness takes place, so many other things stem from it and it becomes a big ball of mess. You find yourself in a turmoil of pain. It hinders the plan and move of God in your life. It was a stronghold that I needed to be loosed from. God was coming to my rescue though I didn't understand. Sometimes, the pain and turmoil seemed unbearable.

This was such a critical point in my life and in my marriage. My husband was not working at the time we had two kids and no income. On top of that, I was going through a midlife crisis. I was also so hurt and broken. It hurt to the core of me and I didn't understand why and how church folk could be so cruel. One person, I did everything in my power to be her friend, and she would consistently talk about me, crack jokes about my lips. She always did it in front of people. I kept going around her because I wanted to be accepted to fit in and no matter how hard I tried it just never worked. When you are broken, wounded and filled with rejection, self-rejection you tend to cleave to people that don't mean you any good. I wanted to be like them, fit in with them. They were having fun, and my life seemed boring like I was missing out on something, (trick of the enemy). I was around my husband, his family and a few saints they were connected to. Whenever we were together, all we did was pray. Besides the praying, we talked about the word and some of them preached to us as we were the audience. My husband and his sister was the main preachers I never did that part. I was intimidated by them because I thought they were above me. Nevertheless, we always had a good time when we all got together. I learned a lot from being around my husband's family and that was no matter what you go through in life pray and keep praying. No matter what life looks like keep pushing and keep pressing. We had our ups and downs, but that's what I gain from them. I know I was messed up with resentment in so many areas in my life. Forgiveness seemed far and impossible. I had so much resentment from feeling of abandoned by my father. Him no being a part of my life for so many years growing up messed me up. I was damaged deeply, and those wounds manifested in every relationship in my life. It was hard for me to receive love from others I wouldn't let anyone get that close to my heart. I was afraid they would abandon me as well leave me hanging out to dry. Truth be told, I was just messed up. I was young, married with children trying to figure this thing out called life. I desired to love and be loved but didn't know how to give it or receive it. The walls around my heart were built up strong. My attitude was bad. I didn't really see it though. In my eyes, I thought I was a sweet person. I did have a mean streak and if you crossed me the wrong way, I would surely show it.

My life was what so many thought they were identifying as an emotional roller coaster; it was up and down. I felt isolated and alone for so long in my life from a little girl into my adult life. I felt unworthy to be loved or that I even mattered. I had low self-esteem. Shame and guilt filled my already heavy and wounded heart. Resentment seemed like a never-ending story. It appeared to be everywhere I went. I had resentment in my heart from past, present and it was creeping into my future. It had a stronghold on me, and though I didn't really understand it all or what was truly going on with me. I knew God was going to show up some way somehow.

Chapter Five

A Grasp On Life

I had two boys and was now pregnant with my third child. How could I be so careless? I definitely didn't plan on having another child so soon. I mean my 2nd son was only 6 ½ months old when I found out. I was devastated when the doctors came in the room and told me I was pregnant. I cried and cried I just did not accept it at all. I called my husband and he knew right away. For the first few months of pregnancy, I did not accept that I was pregnant. I was angry about it. The boys were still young I was experiencing a whole lot in my life and marriage. Having another baby at that moment was bad timing.

September had come and my husband had to go out of town because his grandma had passed away. I was told I couldn't go because there was not enough room for me and the boys.

I was really experiencing rejection at that moment and time. I knew what I felt and saw and nothing else could cover up the real reason behind me not being able to go. I guess I was that bad for him. I was a good wife when I let him go. I didn't feel like the boys and I were important at all. But that was ok. Things were bound to take a turn in life, soon.

My husband left to go out of town for the funeral and the boys and I stayed home. I was three months pregnant with no license and only a permit to drive. My husband left the keys to the car his sister let him get. They told me not to drive the car. The next day when I got up, I was feeling a little ill and decided to drive. Upon getting in the car, the Lord spoke to me clearly and said buckle the kids in correctly. I did just that and that would soon save their lives and mine. I got into the car to drive and within 2 minutes we had crashed. I ran smacked dead into a house and missed hitting a tree by a few inches. The car was totaled. I remember everything being a blur at the hospital and the doctors telling me I had a small hemorrhage in the lining of my belly. The boys and I were not hurt. My neck was badly cut up from the seatbelt but other than that we were all okay. Talk about God having His hand on you He spared all three of our lives. The baby was not out of the woods and the doctors monitored me from then on.

Now, I had to make the dreadful call to my in-laws about the accident. I was fearful because I already knew the outcome of the call. I got a hold of them told them and from there it was about to be another rip through the heart. When they got back, my husband and I got into it that night. He got his things and his video game and left the boys and me and went with his mother house. I think that was the last straw for me. I got my two boys, called some family in Chicago and left on the Greyhound bus. My husband didn't know I left. But when he found out, he tracked me down in Chicago. They were calling me saying you need to get home to your husband. You mean to tell me the same man that walked out on me and my two boys? I didn't think so. I started ignoring their calls and listened to my family who for the first time was actually trying to be there, or so I thought. A few days went by I was still there, until I got a call from my son god mom who I looked up to so much. She prayed with me told me she was there and everything was going to be alright. She told me to come home and because of her, I did just that. It was not because of anything else. When I got home things were still the same. It was the same old talk and so forth. Then a call came in that I would carry for years. I was told if I were someone else my husband would have left me. I received a whole bunch of opinions again that were void of God's word. I then would spend the next day 6 hours being prayed for during this time. I felt scolded and bruised even more.

I felt tortured hearing over and over again saying, "Ronisha, you're the problem. You're holding up your marriage. You are hindering his growth." I wasn't a good example to my kids. I did this for 6 hours. I'll never forget that experience. I just cried on the floor for hours because I didn't want to be that person one of them was speaking about. It made me feel like I was a curse. I was this horrible person who was destroying another man's ministry and dreams. Now that I am wiser and older God would never make you feel so small you feel hopeless. Even in His chastisement, it's done in love and it's rewarding. God is not an accuser, but He builds up and loves with unconditional love.

I survived that. I rested for a few days. I remember being so drained. It was like the life had been sucked out of me. Although I was always the focus, God and I knew the truth about everything going on in my home and my life. For all of you, that's reading this going through similar things. Hold on to God and His word and what He is saying about you. I was still going through life pregnant and not accepting it, but things were about to change. I was about to get a grasp on this thing called life.

I was now five months pregnant and was at my ultrasound appointment. As I laid on my back and she began to exam my stomach she said do you want to know the sex of the baby? She was sure she could see it. I looked at her and said, "Yes." She said, "Well you will need lots of pink." I was having a girl. When she said that, my heart melted and for the first time in 5 months a fire sparked inside of me. I was so happy I was having a baby girl. I was so happy that day and joy filled my heart. She was all I thought about as I was leaving the Drs. Office. I told my husband and a few other people and after that, I just started thinking and reflecting on my life. I didn't want to bring her into this world and I was messed up. I wanted to be the best example to her. I wanted her to have the life I never had or was given that meant I needed to change. In spite of how I was feeling toward my husband or anyone else, I had made up in my mind to try and really start letting go. When things came up, or my husband did something I wouldn't argue or do anything. The next four months was the most peace we had in our marriage since being married. I paid no attention to his hours of being consumed with the computer or Christian chat rooms. I was quiet and mellow. I just wanted what was best for her, my unborn daughter. That year Christmas was at its best. I was showing and glowing and things seem to be looking up, I was working on a better me. We truly enjoyed the holidays that year. My mom gave me another baby shower and I got all the stuff I needed and wanted. I bought so much pink for her. I was just too happy to be having my little girl. I didn't even have a name for her yet. I was just too happy. I think I was finally getting a grasp on life and was calming down from all the yelling and being so angry. I mean I was actually trying. January had come and I had gone into preterm labor. They stopped the labor. I was 5 centimeters dilated I stayed that way for three weeks with three epidurals. At 34 weeks they stopped all medications and let me go into labor with the NICU right there to take my baby. I was in labor but didn't feel a thing. Before you knew it, I was laying there and the baby's head was right there. The nurse said, please don't push until the doctor gets here she was coming out, one push and she was here. She came in weighing 4lbs 4 oz. She was a tiny little fighter. I didn't even get to see her. She was taken right away to the neonatal intensive care unit for babies. I had to wait hours until my epidural wore off to get wheeled up to see her. When I finally laid eyes on her, she had a feeding tube and some oxygen and that's all she needed. I decided right then and there to breastfeed because I wanted her to beat the odds and have a better chance at life. My daughter was a fighter. She only stayed in the hospital seven days and came home with no complications. When she came home, she was weighing 3lbs 12oz. But she was healthy. I loved every inch of her. She was worth the wait and the fight to have her here. She ate every two hours. She ate half an ounce because she was so small. I was protective of her and so much in love with my baby girl. She caused a change in me and I am forever grateful for God's timing on having her.

While I was pregnant with her, I was told by two certain people I need to get my tubes tied and not have any more children. One person at the church said I needed to because of my husband and the other was because of me. I did just that because, at the time in my life, I lived and did what I was told. I thought it would make me a better me. To this day I hate that I ever listened to them because where my marriage is now it far greater than their small narrow minds could even think. They only saw the issues at hand not seeing past to where God was taking us. What we endured all was a part of God's master plan for our lives. Never allow what someone else think dictate your life decisions, trust God in all things. Seek His guidance and listen to His instructions.

Now with three kids and no income we moved a few times until we got settled in a new house. No one ever stayed at the Edmund home. It was a beautiful three story, 3-bedroom house that I loved so much. We moved in with no furniture for a few months and then bought some brand-new furniture and beds for the kids. My husband started barber school, and I had landed a job at ATT formerly known as Cingular. I was making some decent money, the boys were in school, and

From The Hospital To The Pulpit

my daughter was still young. She was not in school. I worked for a while then had to quit working due to not having a sitter. My husband was still in Barber school, he needed to finish. So, I made ends meet for us to survive. When he finished school, he landed a job at a barber shop that he grew in his craft fast. We were still going through our little fights but not as bad as they used to be.

Although we had our issues, all the young people at church surrounded themselves around us. We had prayer at our house all the time and many sleepovers. We prayed many young people through at our house and spent countless hours with them. My heart was toward God, but I had so much built up on the inside of me. Although I was encouraging and praying others through, I didn't believe I was good enough to be healed. Even though we are all undeserving of God's love and favor, I truly didn't believe I could be healed or made whole. I wanted to be just didn't have enough faith to act upon it.

My kids were getting bigger, and my husband was doing well as a barber. We had by now left the church we had been at since I was 18 and started going to church in Brooklyn Park. I just had a huge blow to my heart from church folk and still had not been healed from all the other wounds. I found relief and peace of mind being away from there. Going to the church in Brooklyn Park, I was about to get a huge eye opener. I took some classes at church in Brooklyn Park that shed some light on myself. The class dealt with order and protocol in the church and for the first time, I saw some of my ways were wrong and I too was in error. I reflected on situations I had been in at the Temple and realized I could have done some things a little different. I am not excusing the fact that it was ok for how they treated my family and me because it was all wrong. Being away from all the things and people that caused me pain was a breath of fresh air. I didn't have to deal with that anymore. I didn't have to worry about how they viewed me as a wife and a mother. It was just a huge sigh of relief. My husband and I didn't have that crutch to lean on in our marriage. If something happened, we just had to get through it on our own.

I had been in a car accident in May of 2009, and that money helped us get by for a while. We were able to pay our bills and do the necessary things we needed to. I went through a lot with that accident, but it paid off in the end. We were living in Burnsville at this particular time and driving all the way to Brooklyn Park for church. It was finally just my husband, me and our three kids. No one was there to add their two cents of an opinion in our marriage, my life or our children. My life had been full of that for the past ten years, and I was getting pretty fed up. I longed for the day God would

From The Hospital To The Pulpit

deliver me from the opinions of other people. I know one thing was for sure I was not going out my way to try and please everyone.

Chapter Six

The Question of Why

My husband had been praying and seeking the Lord about what to do concerning church and our family. Upon seeking God, he felt lead to go back to our old church, now why was he doing that I thought. I was crushed. I didn't want to go back. In fact, I now hated that place of worship I once called home. In a few weeks, we moved to Woodbury and started going back to our old church. I was baffled and upset about the whole decision. When we started going back, I made up in my mind to keep to myself. I wasn't about to hang out or get involved with anyone there. I struggled for a few weeks being there. When we walked through the doors, I was already praying for the time to pass for service to be over. Seeing certain faces made my skin cringe and I was one miserable sister. I kept my kids close to me as well. I didn't let them do much at all and I stuck close to my husband. Then it happened. God started dealing with my heart and letting me know this was going to work out for my good. I just had to trust him in this. I had started beauty school and was getting my life in order.

From The Hospital To The Pulpit

Well, at least that's what I thought. I knew I had a lot of issues, but things had gotten better for my family and me. So, now I was back at our former church, I am in school full time, and my husband was doing fairly well at the barber shop. I knew one thing God was dealing with me on. I was to forgive a fellow minister at the church. I As God dealt with me, I didn't want to carry this in my heart anymore. I wanted to be right before God, and she sure was not worth my peace, joy, and happiness. I had to do the unthinkable. I wrestled with God over this, and that was to apologize to her. I'm thinking God you want me to do that and she did all manner of evil toward me? But, me apologizing wasn't for her it was for me. I finally got the strength to do it. I pulled her to the side and I sincerely apologized to her. When I did, it was like a huge weight lifted off me. I was released from that day. And no matter what she did from that day on it no longer mattered to me because God released me from that. I genuinely love her as my sister in Christ. I turned her over to God and kept her in prayer. She was never my issue, to begin with. All along God was trying to work something out of me. She was just the utensil used to bring glory to God's name in my life. When I finally got over that, I got over the opinions of others at church. I just stopped caring about what they had to say about me. I kept to myself. I did get back in the choir and praise team because I loved singing and praising God. Also, while I was there, I got back into ministry. I had stepped down a few years back because I allowed what other people thought of me influence that decision. I also didn't want to be bitter, angry anointed and dysfunctional in ministry so I stepped down. But I was free enough and had enough strength to stick to what God has called me to be and do. I was back in ministry, singing on the praise team and in beauty school full time. Doing Beauty school full time was definitely a sacrifice for me. I went six days a week. It was from Mon- Sat. From 8-4pm. I experienced some highs and lows with school, but my mind was set on finishing and working at my dream job. Upon finishing school, I was one point away from graduating with honors. The only reason I didn't is that I didn't report being hired at JUUT before graduating. My grade was 95.5 I needed 96 for honors, I didn't care. I was just excited to be done with school and starting the career of my dreams. My graduation ceremony was in June. I was finished with school in May 2012. I was due to start JUUT in July, but they pushed it back to August 24th, 2012. I had the rest of the summer to enjoy before starting work.

The summer of 2012 was like no other. Things were falling into place. Our mentors from the church were heading up a new ministry in Apple Valley. I was sure going with them. My husband and our mentor was very close and connected spiritually.

From The Hospital To The Pulpit

Before I could even say anything, my husband said we were going with them as they start a new ministry. You see with all the "Why" questions I had before God; He had it all worked out from the start. If we hadn't gone back to the church, we would have missed the timing of God and being able to start with them in ministry at the new place. We had our first service in April 2012 a month shy of me graduating, and it couldn't have come at a better time in life.

Things were looking up a fresh start, I felt is strong.

I'm now done with school waiting to start my job I had a high-end apartment I mean things were looking good. I spent the summer just cruising through life enjoying where I was at that point in my life. The kids and I did stuff together. I loved church and my life at this point, but something was about to happen that brought up the feeling inside again.

It was my husband's birthday and I threw him a party. I took time out to celebrate him and when it was over the enemy crept right in. I fell out with family over something that baffled me to this day. When that happened, everything changed. Though we all still said hi and everything, things changed me. I didn't view our relationship the same from that day on. It hurt to the core; I don't think I got over it. I stopped going over as much and slowly, but surely the distance became more and more frequent.

It came time to start my job, and I remember the first week of training we talked about The Be, Do, Have. Be intentional, do, show action and have results. I remember the instructor telling her story about her stepchild, and that resonated with me. Things were beginning to come to light. I stopped trying to please anyone and would be intentional about being myself. I decided that day to let go of the situation and give it to God. I decided to put the relationships in His hands. It amazed me how many positive relationships I had at Juut in a short span of time. It felt like family every day I went to work. I enjoyed every moment of it. I was thriving at work, and my confidence was high for the time being.

I actually believed in myself for once. The kids were doing well in school. I mean what more could I ask for in life. From August 24th, 2012 to December 31st, 2012, I was on an upscale pace in life.

That was all about to change in four days and take me on a journey that would land me right where I am today. This is why I am writing this book and these words to you.

From The Hospital To The Pulpit

Remember when going through your process, trust God. Be intentional about your healing, deliverance and breakthrough. Never measure yourself based off someone's inability to see who you are. Take no thought for yourself and God will take thought for you. He is the author and finisher of your faith. What I am about to share is the part that birth the glory behind my story. Everything I went through brought me into my now. I am grateful for every test, trial and affliction. It brought me into a true relationship with God. This was a real death walk to kill off my flesh and everything concerning me. I still living daily dying to myself. Every day there will always be something to surrender to the cross. God is my refuge, my help and my father. I am nothing without Him.

Chapter Seven

The Critical Hour

January 4th of 2013 changed my life forever. I got up like any ordinary day for work, although I was feeling sick and felt tightness in my chest. I still continued with my day for work, I just loved being there. Upon arriving at work, I checked my books for the day and prepared my station for my first guest who was my boss. I did a blowout on her, but I barely made it through it. After finishing, I made my way upstairs to their office. My chest was so tight. I was feeling faint as well. My boss must have sensed it because after finishing her hair, she went up to clear my books for the rest of the day. As soon as I made it to their office, they called 911. I was rushed to Methodist Hospital. Upon arriving, I remember going in and out of consciousness. I was intubated for the first time in my life. The doctors placed me in the critical care unit of ICU. I stayed on a ventilator for four days. I had caught the flu and was in a fight for my life. On the fourth day, I pulled the tube out my mouth. My breathing was stable, so they kept the tube out. I stayed in ICU another day then transferred to another floor in the hospital. The very next day, I realized something was different my weight, I lost 14lbs. I was already a thin person, to begin with. I only weighed 103lbs before getting sick. I noticed my toes felt strange and then I lost feeling in them. I thought it was because I was so sick. The doctors came in and tried to stand me up and my legs collapsed. I thought I was just super weak from the flu. They said they would monitor it and came back the next day and all the feeling in my legs was gone. They immediately rushed me to the operating room for a spinal tap. By the time I got back to my room, they were arranging to send me back for surgery to have a catheter placed in my chest. They told me I had Guillain-Barre Syndrome, a disease where your immune system attacks your nervous system and causes paralysis. I went to the operating room had the catheter placed flowing through the major vein in my heart.

I remember being in so much pain after it was placed because the tube was inserted right at my collar bone. I wanted it taken out, but if I wanted a great chance at getting better, I had to have it. And so it started, the pain medication was given through IV every 15 minutes. I was given morphine to keep me comfortable. I returned to my room to prepare for my treatments to stop the progression of the disease. GBS had progressed and moved up my legs and to the right side of my body. I wasn't scared just yet because in my mind I thought this would pass soon and I would be back to work and living life soon. I stayed in the hospital three weeks before being transferred to rehab that is where reality set in and hit hard.

I remember laying in the bed at rehab it was late, no family, no nurses or doctors just me in a dark room alone. I begin just to weep and this was my first breaking point. God softly spoke to me and said this is between you and me, Ronisha. I knew then that no one could help me and that I had to get this thing for myself. I was sure about to come into a true knowledge of God and who He truly was in my life. The next day I got up for therapy, I had little energy yet I was beginning to sink into a deep hole of depression. I hated the sight of me barely being able to shake your hand and that my speech was altered. My family came most days at rehab. My kids and my job wrote letters of encouragement to me. They hung all over my rehab room to remind me to keep pushing and keep fighting through this. At one point some of the saints came to pray for me and I remember it relieved me but didn't heal me because God was waiting for me to come to him myself. Which lead me through a journey of submitting to God and letting go.

From The Hospital To The Pulpit

Rehab was working, not as fast as I would have liked it too. It took so much out of me just to get up try and do the basic things in life that we all sometimes take for granted. I struggled to hold a toothbrush and just the thought of trying to put it in my mouth and brush was even harder. My muscles were extremely weak and I need assistance to do everything. I could sit up in my wheelchair, but I needed support. It seemed like a never-ending battle. A week into rehab I was rushed back to the hospital because my heart rate was extremely high and so was my blood pressure. I was admitted to the cardiology floor because my heart was in distress. I was really scared and nervous about this. The doctors got me stable and kept me on the cardiology floor for a week to monitor me. Afterward, I was sent back to her complete rehab. I had moved from a dysphasia diet to soft foods. I was getting better. Rehab was so intense we had to be careful not to overdo anything because it could set me back. If I worked my muscles too hard the next day they would crash and we would be back at square one. During this time at rehab, I shed so many tears. I just couldn't understand all that was going on. I remember a former pastor came to visit me and as we sat and talked. He began to pray for me and he told me you will praise dance again. You will sing again and do so much more. I held on to those words and they would at times replay in my head to remind me of

God's word in my life. I can't thank him enough for those words of life.

It was hard being in rehab. I was missing my family I begin to realize I've taken for granted what really mattered most. I wasn't there to see my kids off to school or help with their homework and that crushed me. My kids were going through too they went from seeing me every day and me being a part of their everyday lives to me not being there. My baby hair had falling out. My husband was struggling to keep it together and stay strong for us. He felt helpless to me because he prayed and prayed and fasted, but I was still sick. What do you do when the life you thought you had comes crashing in on you and there is nothing you can do about it? My back was against the wall. I couldn't back up any further in life. The only way out was to look up and push forward. I knew what I had to do, but it was a fight to do it and get there. It was getting close to that time to go home and rehab was setting everything up for me. A doctor entered the room that evening to talk about my discharge. I'll never forget that day. He began explaining the process and then said hypnosis would help me and that with that I could make my legs move with my mind. I got so upset that night and tears flowed down my face because I wanted so bad to walk. He was saying some type of stuff I don't even believe in. So much went on that night and the one person who I believed in that was supposed to have my back, went and told all my personal information to people I specifically asked not to tell my business to. Being sick and going through was personal to me and we weren't that close anymore for him to be doing that. My trust and confidence to confide in my husband was gone from that day and would be another hurdle I would have to get over. Now, feeling all alone with not one person to talk to and be there for me made me feel hopeless. My back was truly against the wall. I was backed up in a corner with nowhere to turn. So now upon discharge, everything was set up for me but when I got home it was a disaster in the house. All I wanted was my kids. I wanted to be around them. They gave me hope and seeing them made me press through and keep fighting.

Transitioning to being at home was hard. Nursing and everything was set up, but the only thing that came through was my therapy. Not being able to do much for myself, my kids had school and my husband was working, I was left home alone for some hours. Everything would be provided by my bed or the couch before they left for the day. It was a tough time; some days the pastor would come and look after me. He would study until the kids, or my husband got home. One particular day, I didn't have much to eat. I couldn't get to any food and I stayed 8 hours on the couch crying until my sister drove from Oak Grove an hour away to bring me food. I hated every moment of going through this.

A week out of rehab I was back in the hospital intubated because some strange things begin to happen with my lungs. I was put on more steroids and a higher dosage inhaler to try and maintain the asthma. I stayed in the hospital three days and went home. That was in March 2013.

April came I was taken back to the hospital and intubated a 3rd time. This time it would alter my life again and cause another dramatic change. After being in the hospital a week I was told if I could walk to the end of the hall, I could go home. I was excited. I was sick of the hospitals now and just wanted to be around my kids. They needed me. My mom and dad were at the hospital at this time. I begin to walk. I started feeling lightheaded and that was all I remembered. I flat-lined right there on the floor. My mom said I scared her so bad. She said she was in my ear saying you better fight. You better wake up. Fight RONISHA. The doctors rushed to my aide, got me stable and placed me in ICU. When I woke up, they said you're not going home. We have to run several more tests to find out what's going on with you. I spent another week in the hospital and things started getting worse. My blood pressure shifted. It went high and my heart rate dropped low then it would go low and my heart rate high. I had severe hypertension. POTS disease was what they diagnosed me with. It just kept getting worse my oxygen levels were starting to drop. Every time I would stand up it dropped. They couldn't figure out why my blood gas levels were low; they ran more tests. They scheduled me for a 6-minute walk test but determined that was too dangerous for me. When they first tried within a minute of walking my oxygen dropped to 57%. It was scary. I know. So, I was now placed on continuous oxygen and more breathing meds, I was very sick at this point in my life. Therapy consisted of me building up endurance to even try and walk. My lungs were so weak and so was my body. I stayed in the hospital for 6 weeks and spent my birthday and Mother's Day there. Reality had truly set in about life and I began to get things right in relationships. I got back in touch with an old friend. We had fallen out over some childhood stuff, but God blessed, we are on good terms as I write. This was really scaring me. Now transitioning back home, I had to make another adjustment to life. I had oxygen and a BiPAP machine. I couldn't breathe without the oxygen machine and needed the BiPAP whenever I slept. Line care set up my oxygen at home. I also went home with my own special made wheelchair. I was going to need it. So now at home, I'm walking and getting around with this oxygen cannula around my face hooked up to a 24ft cord. If I traveled outside the home, I had to bring a couple of oxygen tanks because they didn't last that long. I hated going out people would just stare you down like I was contagious or something. And going to church was the same way at times. People were asking tons of questions or rendering their opinion. It was a struggle adjusting to life now. I felt so lonely, entrapped with all type of emotions. I know I needed God, but it was a struggle to give in, not because He wasn't there but because I just didn't surrender to Him.

I was home a month and was back in the hospital in August and September. By November, it was 18th time I been intubated. I felt so helpless and angry. Depression had drowned me and I stop trying. I just sank into a dark hole and was back and forth to the hospital. I just couldn't see my way out of this and in November I tried to end my life. I took 26 Tylenol, 8 Benadryl pills, and some Nyquil. I was still here they took me to the hospital and they administered some reversal meds through IV. That's all I remember before waking up. I was intubated with a tube down my throat and surrounded by church members. This was tough. Why was I still here? God had mercy on me, that's why. He had a plan for my life. I was just messed up. I stayed in the hospital for a few weeks and then went home. Now, the holidays were here Christmas and my job adopted my family. It was the best Christmas ever. The whole front side of my living room was filled with gifts and they also brought the most beautiful tree. Along with tons of gifts, they gave me over a thousand dollars and also a 300.00 gift card for food. My kids had the best Christmas ever because of my Juut family. They made everything feel normal for us.

Things were about to shift for me after Christmas. I was rushed back to the hospital intubated and placed in ICU. Now back at the University of Minnesota Hospital, I stayed there for two weeks during this stay and intubated three times. I had enough of them and transferred to another hospital only to be intubated again and placed on complete bed rest. I could not sit-up above a 45-degree angle without my blood pressure going dangerously high. I was strictly bed ridden.

There was just so much going on in the hospital. During this time, my husband brought a pastor to come pray for me again and nothing happened. I was still sick but that was about to start changing. I got a visit from my former pastor. We talked about me taking pain meds. I had been on them since I started getting sick. My body was used to taking them and if I didn't it would react to not having them. Everyone was so focused on the meds they fail to deal with my why. When he left, I was angry something stirred up in me and I said I have got to get out this hospital and fight. I was going to prove every accuser wrong about my life. Right before that I was losing my will to fight. I was losing hope and faith and lost trust that I would ever come out of this. I was in a hopeless state. The doctors kept saying I would be in a transitional care facility for a very long time. So I was physically messed up and spiritually tore up. When the Pastor left, I knew I had to push. I was in my room laying on the bed and began crying hard and God spoke to me and said I am here. Right then for the first time since being sick, I begin to truly call on His name and He touched me. I got strength like no other and the fight was on. I starting slowing down on the pain meds but when things got tough, I gave in. It was not because I couldn't overcome but because I didn't want to deal with the reality of life and that I had some real issues. Still laying in the bed on bed rest, I told the doctor I had to go home. The doctors looked at me like I was crazy they said I was too sick to go home and needed to go to a transitional home to be cared for. I wasn't going for that. He came back the next day I said I need to go home now. He said if you can sit up just a little and your blood pressure not fly through the roof, then I'll consider. The doctor said that with assurance that I wasn't going to be able to sit up, but he didn't know the God I served. He called the nurses in to assist me. I said a prayer and they begin to raise the head of my bed little by little. Nothing happened, so they raised it some more and nothing happened. The doctor said to try and sit up. I was believing God because I needed to get home. This was now January 2014. Through prayer and faith in God, I sat up with help and in two days I was going home. I went home on blood thinners and all the rest of my meds. I was okay with giving myself a shot every day as long as I was going home. When I got home, I had already made up in my mind to fight and give it all I had to come out of this. I was still very sick couldn't stand up on my own or anything being bed ridden for a month. It had caused severe deconditioning in my body. My mind was made up though to fight till the finish so at home I begin the process of going through withdrawals from the pain meds. Even though I was in pain, I wanted to trust God. I went cold turkey for two weeks the first week being so bad sweats, chills, and all, but I had a made-up mind. By week two things calmed down a little and I kept pushing and pushing.

During week two, I was home with the kids. I was about to experience God in a way I never had before. I was laying in my room and got a text from my covenant sister in Delaware that I had connected with while I was sick and she told me to watch Juanita Bynum live. I immediately turned it on. On my iPad, I began to watch her preach and she began to explain her encounter with God. I said, Lord, if this is real, I want to experience you.

From The Hospital To The Pulpit

Before I could finish the words, my body flew from one end of the bed to the next. I couldn't move or anything and a scream came out like no other. I went through this for a few hours and the presence that came over me in that room it was unbelievably amazing. My heart was so overwhelmed. I couldn't believe what had just happened to me. God was most definitely real and I just experienced Him for myself. Nothing can ever take that away from me. I have come upon my journey to being made whole. The next day God just starting dealing with me on things and stuff I needed to let go. I cried out to Him. I was at the point where I didn't want to hold on to that stuff anymore. It wasn't worth it in the end. A few days of that and then the former Pastor came over to visit before my husband went to work. We talked and I told him what happened to me. I still couldn't walk at this time. Then we started praying and God once again started dealing with my heart. After prayer, my husband took me to the bathroom and while I was in there, he left. God said stand up. I was scared at first because if that wasn't God and I tried to stand, I was sure going to fall and hurt myself. At that time, I was moving on faith and I knew it was going to take great faith to get me out of this. I stood up wobbly, but then I moved a step. The feeling a joy was overtaking me and I stepped again. I couldn't believe it. I called out to my husband and Pastor and said look. They both said walk and I walked from the bathroom to my room. It took crazy faith to get me to this point on this journey. From that day, I kept pushing and pushing. Though God wasn't done dealing with my heart, it was all about to unfold. A few months went by and I finally was feeling kind of normal I didn't need my oxygen as much anymore. I was getting stronger and stronger. By the summer, I had gained weight was looking healthy and getting back active in life. I started attending church regularly and getting involved again in ministry. By June, I was working the altar again at church and doing what I loved. I was still going through the process and journey of healing. Things begin to unfold in my life and shift my attitude. My hunger for God and my fire for God was coming back. I was in a season of restoration at this time in my life. I had to let everything go. I had to let my family go. All the years of abuse and hurt by them, I had to let them go. I was no longer allowing them or their words to destroy me or hinder me. I believed enough in God and His word and what he said about me. Letting go of all my family cutting all ties with them was the best thing I had ever done. I felt so free and liberated by not being bound by their opinions and cruelty. I was no longer bound by their inability to love and speak kind things to me or anyone else. God had freed me from that and the curse that goes back generations. I started getting into my word. I was praying and fasting and doing the things required of me. I had to forgive all those that hurt me in church and out of the church. I had to give all the heartaches and pain over to the Lord. I didn't want to be bound any longer by unforgiveness. The closer I drew to God the more confident I became in Him and what He thought about me. I was pushing and fighting every step of the way. The more I read the word of God and got it down in my spirit, the more liberated I became. Things were getting better in my home, in my marriage, in my walk with God. It was just amazing to see how God was unfolding things. Everything He had spoken to me down through the years was about to manifest right before my eyes. The summer had passed and the kids were getting ready to go back to school. I had to have an emergency surgery to remove my appendix. I stayed in the hospital a couple of days and went home.

God was not finished with me yet. By November my husband's father had fallen very ill and he would spend the next few months visiting his dad and being by his side. For the first time in my life, I felt empty without him, but I know he had to be with his dad. I encouraged him to go and be there as much as possible. As I was home the turning in my heart was still taking place, things I thought was of value to me no longer was. I still had a way to go on this journey but my mind was completely made

From The Hospital To The Pulpit

up and my heart was fixed on Jesus. While my husband was gone, I used that time to spend with the Lord continuing to allow Him to work out things in me. I knew when my husband got back, he would need all our love and support. December, we didn't really have together because I wanted my husband to spend as much time with his dad as he could. The kids and I didn't go and that's was ok with me. By the end of December, my husband's dad passed and he had to leave again to lay him to rest. I had surgery and was recovering. My body could not endure the long drive to Mississippi, so I stayed home and just did what I had to do praying for my husband and his family. My husband had to preach at his dad's funeral and because of my religious state of being from what I had been taught throughout the years, I didn't think he should have done it. But while I was talking to him on the phone God let me know He was in it and I encouraged my husband and told him to let the Lord use him. We prayed and God moved on him as he preached his dad's home going service. The beauty of all this was the amazing life change God did in his father. I was in awe of being able to witness the power of God in that man's life and now he is resting with the Lord. When my husband got back, we cleaved to one another so tight for the first time in our marriage. We knew what mattered most, God first and each other. The New Year had started January 2015 and all though things were turning for me in my health and healing journey. My husband was grieving hard. I needed to be there for him. My heart was fixed on him making sure he didn't sink into depression. I tried as much as I could just to be there, love him and pray. I was still getting stronger day by day and God was unfolding things in my life. His word was coming alive and bringing about a supernatural transformation. Our Anniversary was approaching and we were in a better place. We spent our day together went to eat and enjoyed one another's company. This was a time where I was about to enter into a shift in my life. The next day I was asleep, in my sleep I start hearing we don't have time and it repeated over and over. When I woke up, it repeated. God was speaking this to me. I got my iPad and began to write and study and the message filled my heart. Later that day, I got a call that I would be preaching for the very first time April 18th, 2015. That was my very first message, "We Don't Have Time." I begin fasting went on consecration for 18 days that was up until the day I preached. I never imagined God to move in the manner that He did and from there God was shifting in me. I was on a takeoff in God. The more I prayed, the more I got into the word of God, the more I yearned for Him. You see the thing I love about God is that He spoke this about me when I was a little girl and again when I got saved. When you are going through, you don't see it. Sometimes, people that are right in your midst don't see it because they are looking at your condition and not the conclusion. People may write you off, say you don't matter and you're not called or not qualified. The devil is a liar. To you that are reading my book right now, God will turn your mess into a message and your tragedy into a triumph. Hold on to the promises God has spoken concerning your life, and never give up. I am a living witness that God doesn't call the qualified He qualifies the called. He specializes in rejects, people that are outcast and so forth. I was pushed to the side for years, told I didn't matter and rejected right in the house of God. God had His hand on my life from the very beginning. So back to my journey, I preached April 18th, 2015. I was 33 years old. God indeed had His way I am forever grateful. Oh no don't think the enemy wasn't sitting back waiting to peek his ugly head in. We had relocated to Apple Valley to be closer to church and to upgrade our living space. We moved May 1st, 2015 and got the kids all settled. I was still growing in ministry. I was now over the children's dance ministry and that was going well. Then, boom I have my first encounter at church with some saints. That day I almost walked away from that place of worship I did not want to go back into anything that had me bound once before. My birthday was spent broken and crying out to God. I didn't even want to celebrate it. I'm still going through the journey of healing now. I got a call from an amazing sister who talked with me and prayed with me. She understood where I was and was not about to let me just sit. Also, one of the young ladies I use to mentor just went out and did the unthinkable she got me a cake and gifts came over sang Happy Birthday to me with my family. It was a priceless moment, a memory I will never ever forget and always cherish. So the next day God really begin to deal with me about what it meant to serve and be a leader. I had to number one let that mess go it was not worth my peace and joy. I wasn't even playing the blame game. I just said work on me as your servant. Even though I know, I didn't do what I was accused of I apologized because at the end of the day I wanted to please God in every way. At this point in my life, I was just ready and my heart was turning to God. God was bringing me to a place of humility and meekness. I'm not going to tell you that feels good either because it doesn't. I had to submit to what God was doing and working out in my life. It hurt, it crushed me to the core of my being but it was all worth it in the end.

Chapter Eight

The Journey

Some issues had come up with my eldest son at middle school. Now before moving to Apple Valley, my son was thriving in school. He began to struggle and was being bullied at school and he just wouldn't fight or stand up for himself. My heart was being ripped seeing him go through this and as a mother you never want to see your child suffer. I began questioning if it was even the right move to Apple Valley. We didn't like it at all. Every time I would think about moving, God would speak to me and say hold on, I had to wait. I knew moving to Apple Valley was not the will of the father. Being out of God's will shipwrecked our family. I was glad the summer had arrived. My son could get a break from all the drama surrounding the school. We spent our summer together. I became a pro at barbecuing and doing fun things with my family. Then in July, my husband had another shift in barbershops and that would take a turn in our finances for the good.

From The Hospital To The Pulpit

It's was approaching again when I would have to preach again. The date was July 18th. There was something about those 18's. This time our former church was coming to hear me preach. They heard about the first time I preached and wanted to support me. The church was packed, but for some reason, it never moved me. I was centered on God and what he had for me. My message was "Come forth" dealing with Lazarus and coming out of grave clothes. In fact, God was unfolding that in my very own life. He was bringing me out of dead clothes and bringing me forth in Him. God really moved that night in service and I am so very grateful that He did. I could feel the hand of God turning things around. He was turning my mess into a message. God was peeling back the layers in my life and I was open and ready for Him to do so.

August approached, I was at church and boom, I got sick again. I was rushed off to the hospital by ambulance. It got bad on the way. They pulled over on the side of the road and intubated me. This was my 45th time being intubated now. I don't remember anything except within the next few days when they took the tube out. I was gradually coming out of sedation. While in ICU, I sat and pondered on how could this be? I thought I was over all this and frustration set in. But then a fight and determination came right behind it. I had come too far to give up now. Then it hit again, my legs got weak and my muscles gave out. It was a total disaster. I had been diagnosed with a rare disease called Mitochondrial Cytopathy, and Myopathy and it was aggressive for me. It could come at any time without warning and raise havoc in my life. So now, I hear the doctors say you're very ill and you need to also start therapy again to slow down the weakness in my muscles. I sat in that hospital bed. I said, God, I'm coming out of this and I'm coming out for good. A fight welled up inside me and I was ready no matter what. A few days later, I was transferred to the rehab floor at the hospital and I was so weak, but in my mind I was strong. I rested that day to prepare for therapy the following day. They came to my room. The therapy started in my room first. I was too weak to leave it. But I pressed through. It was hard and I shed a lot of tears that day. The first few days, I was doing therapy in my room and then I started going to the therapy gym to work on my muscles. It was so hard at times. I had to scream through it because the pain would be so unbearable, but I kept pushing. I kept fighting. One day after a long day of therapy, I was in my room and the Lord spoke to me and said you must obey Me in all things. God wanted every piece of me, not just half of me. I just wept and wept and then a strong release and sense of peace came over me. I had my husband bring me some headphones for therapy the next day. I put my praise and worship on and I begin to work while having the faith to come out. I didn't look at my current condition, but I saw myself every day walking up out that hospital. I prayed and prayed and spoke over myself and declared the healing of the Lord over my life. I began to improve in what would have taken months only took a few weeks. God was turning things around fast. I was finally strong enough to go home and when I got there, I knew the battle wasn't over. I was still weak. I was getting stronger but still needed assistance. My health care was set up at home and the nurse came three days a week and therapy was set to continue at home as well. Three times my nurse came and I had to call 911 because of my grave condition, but I kept believing God. I kept fighting. I was not accepting the report of the doctors. As I surrounded myself with prayer day by day, I got stronger and stronger and before you know it, I was moving about again starting to feel like my old self. But my life was about to shift in a dramatic way and it was all in the plan of God. As God began to move and strengthen me in my body, I begin to really push. I moved on what we call ridiculous faith. I just couldn't see myself staying in that situation. Even in my present condition at that time God was molding me and shaping me and showing me myself. I still needed some healing and deliverance and this was soon about to grip the very core of my heart. As I got well, God constantly had situations before me that showed me how much I really needed Him and needed to be made whole. There were two particular things I had been in denial of for years and that was depression. Although I knew it was there, I ignored it and pretended like it did not exist in my life. One thing I have learned is that we have to be honest with God about where we are and when He reveals things to us, we have to face it and allow Him to heal and deliver us. I didn't do that for years and at this point in my life, I was embarrassed to admit I had depression. Depression is a silent killer and to me a deadly killer. It robs you of true joy down on the inside. It was about to come to a head and God was in the process of making me whole in Him. As I began to get back into my daily routine of life and being busy with church and all the duties there, God was working on me. I remember being in my prayer closet and God speaking to me saying remain faithful no matter what. That word I would need to hold on to the very next week as I found myself being in a situation where my faith was tested at church. I found myself being more concerned about me and how I felt about a situation versus relying on God and trusting He knew what was best for me. I saw that I still had some growing up to do. When we say I am working for you God, the question is are we really or for the approval of man or a pastor. Everything we do must be done as unto to the Lord with a spirit of excellence. Col 3:23 And whatsoever ye do, do it heartily, as unto the Lord, and not unto man. Daniel had a spirit of excellence in Daniel 6:3.

I had to take my eyes completely off people including my pastor and focus on me and what God was doing on the inside. Everything I do I must do it as unto the Lord. God was cleaning me up from the inside out. Sometimes, we make things about us when it's really not it's to help bring someone else out of what they are in. I had to remember that along the way and no matter what happens, remain faithful to God first. God's hand was turning inside my heart and I could feel it. It was starting to be noticeable. I was active in the church and a lot of things. I became a youth leader at the end of 2015. I was over the intercessory pray line at 5:30 am in the morning. I was over both dance ministries, along with preaching, teaching and balancing life out with my own family. I was very busy in church yet in the process God was working on me from the inside out. I was about to be hit with a situation that brought everything to a head in my life. My eldest son was getting out of control at home and school. He was failing his classes and getting into all type of stuff. It was also rubbing off on the middle son and our home was about to be shaken. Here I was helping other youth and my own kids were falling. How could that be? I was not about to sit back and allow the devil to steal, kill and destroy my own children. One day the enemy

From The Hospital To The Pulpit

came in hard and both sons found themselves running away. I just found myself hitting the floor and crying out to God. He was the only one that could turn the situation around. But in prayer, God showed me myself in the problem. He showed me what was going on in my home. I had overstepped my boundaries as a wife by not letting my husband discipline the boys and be there as their father. Whenever something happened, I never stood in agreement with him and wives that are reading this that's not a price you will want to pay. As God opened my eyes, I cried out for forgiveness and asked God for help and wisdom in the situation. And He came right on in and worked things out for me. My husband got home that night and I allowed him to not only be the head but to be a father to our three children. I took the pants off and never put them back on. I didn't want them at the price of losing my kids and having a chaotic home. I wanted God more than I wanted to be in control. I submitted to him in that and allowed God to be in control of our home, marriage, and children. We prayed that night in our home and God came right in. From that day the tables have turned greatly. My son went from public school to homeschool and from making D's in school to straight A's. Things came in order as God designed for them to for family. Ephesians 5:22 Wives, submit yourselves unto your own husbands, as unto the Lord. That's the word of God, not my words and I have found that it is far greater to do so as unto the Lord. You're doing it as unto the Lord seeing it that way will help you do it more and more if you are seeking to please God. The overwhelming peace that fills my home is amazing because it is built on the principles and foundation of the word of God. God was transforming me from the inside out and I was grateful. I survived that situation. God's grace and mercy carried me through. God was peeling off the layers from the inside out. I still had these two issues to face. The two were depression and the other I will name when I get to it. I finally decided that I needed an outlet. I didn't have anyone to talk to about my childhood or the issues that ripped through the core of my heart. I was ready to give it all over to God and truly surrender my all not just some of me to Him, but all of me. I got connected with a lady who was a therapist and a saved, a Pastor and born-again believer. I knew I couldn't talk to anyone at church they wouldn't even understand me if I did anyways. So I took a leap of faith and started going. I truly believe you need to be healed spiritually and emotionally and mentally. There needs to be balance. In all three areas, I know God was bringing balance and stabilizing me in it. The first couple of meetings was breaking the ice, in the fourth, it came up. The big word depression was addressed. I wept like a baby on the couch talking to her. When I got in the car, I wept. I began to declare the word of God over me.

From The Hospital To The Pulpit

Finally, I was facing it head on and it wasn't easy, but I was determined to be made whole. When I got home, I made an appointment with a now former pastor and went over there the following day. The deliverance of the Lord began to flow. I wasn't about to allow that to rip through my life or rob me of my future. When I left three hours later, I felt a ton of bricks lifted off my heart. That was truly a place I had longed for in my life for many years. The journey to wholeness had truly begun. I continued on my walk with God and seeing my life therapist. She was amazing to me and breath of fresh, liberating air. I could hardly wait for our sessions and even the painful ones I was determined to come out and be whole. My mind was made up.

Well, my 16th Year anniversary was approaching I had struggled through the years in my marriage with giving my husband all of me. Because of being molested since age four, it tore me in ways and areas that were robbing me of my future. I longed to be healed but didn't know how to be or to be set free. I wanted to please him as his wife but I couldn't. Those feelings would consume me and I would shut down. But one day in therapy, we dealt with the situation. We did some breathing techniques. My therapist said you are cleansed by the blood. You are blood washed, in Jesus name. She told me to declare that I am cleansed by the blood of Jesus, and my past no longer had a hold on me. Shame and guilt would no longer grip my heart and body. I began driving home declaring the word of God over my life and my body. I was pleading the blood of Jesus over it and confessing that I am cleansed through His blood. The more I declared it, the more I felt His power come in wash me over that day. I knew that day God had broken the shame and guilt off my life and I was free from the bondage of it. My Anniversary had approached and I would see how much God set me free. I can say that day I enjoyed every bit of my husband and it was the most amazing feeling in the world. I had overcome years of torment and guilt and I was so amazed at the power of God flowing in my life. The more God moved, the more it gave me a hunger and thirst for Him. I craved God and wanted to please Him. My life was about to shift again in another two days. I was about to go on a fast that would shift the very being of my life. It began on April 1st, 2016 and would last until May 11th, 2016, two days before my birthday. My first two days of the fast God came in mightily. On Saturday at church, things would change in my life. While in church praising God. He filled my mother with the Holy Ghost with the evidence of speaking in tongues. God did what I had been praying for. One thing I know is that when you delight yourself in the Lord, He will give you the desires of your heart. It was the most amazing thing to look at her and see what God was doing. My mother was truly crying out to God and God was transforming her life right before our eyes. Seeing that gave me excitement about pursuing God and dedicating my whole life to Him. The fast I was on consisted of the first ten days of liquid only after 4 pm. I survived that because this was a God lead fast. During the first ten days, God began to deal with me and He gave me a prophetic word that He was sending His wind. I was about to preach on April 9th, 2016. There was a shift in my life and ministry that day and I don't think I will ever be the same. God came in greatly in the service and filled a young person with the Holy Ghost. I came home ready to give God my all. He was doing something amazing on the inside on me and I was grateful. On that Sunday after 6 pm and ten days after eating no food. I took my first meal. The fast would consist of 1 meal at 6 pm for the next two weeks then end with liquid only again after 4 pm. God is so faithful in all that He showed me during this fast and all He has used my hands to do. I am writing this book while still on this fast and these past few days have been quite interesting. What I am about to share is a journey that I am on toward complete healing and restoration in God. I had been seeing a therapist for the past six weeks mainly to get over my traumatic childhood. I know I haven't touched on that much, but that's part of my journey and I believe sharing it will set many free who are bound up.

My innocence was taken from me at the age of four. I was molested countless times, and it continued as I got older. The abuse also happened from my cousins who would molest and touch me all over. They would take my clothes completely off and have sex with me. One of my girl cousins would do this over and over to me penetrating my vagina with her fingers. It was horrible. I went through this for years and I remember moving to Minnesota thinking it would stop, but it continued. I remember having to stay with relatives because my mom didn't have a place yet when we moved to Minnesota in 1989. My sister and I was jumped on and molested by our girl cousins. Some days it would be just fighting us and we would not fight back at first. Until one day, I got tired of being jumped on and when I fought back it gave me some confidence. I was fighting ever since.

By the fourth grade, I was still being molested by my girl cousin for about another year then it stopped. The damage was already done. By the sixth grade, I had started rebelling against my mom. I hardly ever wanted to be home and always made plans with my friends. My mom had her place by then and was doing fairly well with what she had. She always made sure we had food to eat and every holiday she made sure we enjoyed it. I had learned by then to mask the past, bury it deep inside me and to never think of it, but that little girl could not stay hidden long as I said in previous chapters. She came out at a horrible time. I never knew how to deal with it or get the help I needed. Even on the journey of healing from rejection, abandonment, bitterness and forgiveness, I never dealt with what transpired as a child. The Lord was leading me on a path to complete healing from it all. I knew I not only had to be healed spiritually but emotionally as well. That would take me to the road of seeing my therapist every Monday. It was tough at first admitting that I needed help. But I had to let go of pride and do what I needed to do to be made whole. The first few weeks of therapy was just getting to know me then at six weeks it started getting rough. We started digging deep into my past and that sparked some emotions I had buried for so long. To be heal you must first admit you have a problem and you need God. You had to face it head on. No matter how painful and scary it may seem, you must face it, deal with it and allow God to heal you. I began for the first time in 34 years to face my fear, my problems and deal with them as they came up in therapy. My first one was facing my first encounter at four years old. I didn't know that I had it hidden so deeply, but I had to face it to get over it. I began to deal with it and I found for me I needed help dealing with it. Not everyone will have to do this. Each person is different and I say be led by the Spirit of God as you go through your journey of healing. I had to be temporarily put on depression meds just to help me cope with getting through my pain of my traumatic childhood. Dealing with it, I thought I didn't need any meds but the feelings were all too overwhelming and I felt myself sinking. I was getting them and would take them until the difficult part of this journey was over. One thing that helps me fight through this is a made-up mind, determination and my faith in God. Knowing that He is with me every step of the way and that I'm coming out, kept my faith stable. A few days after my therapy session, I was having a really hard time and I began to ask what was the purpose of me going through so much as a child and into my adult life? When I went to bed that night, the Lord gave me a dream, and in that dream, He told me I was right where He wanted me and that everything was ok. He then showed me tons and tons of names just flashing before me and said many would be set free because of my testimony and me sharing and writing this book. Whoever is reading this, know that there is hope in God that you can come out and be made whole. It's not about becoming a survivor because I did that for many years. I just survived through life. I learned to do that well. But I was about to move from a survivor to an

OVERCOMER in Christ. There is a huge difference. A survivor is just that. You survived the horrific events, but it still have power over you. It robs you of your joy and peace and the ability to live in the abundance that God has for you. My past was not about to have a grip on my future or present life no longer. I was about to be an OVERCOMER. I would be free and at liberty to live my life in the abundance and overflow of God. I tell you don't give-up keep pushing, keep fighting keep praying and trusting and believing God. He will never leave or forsake you. His promises are true. His word is yea and amen 2 Corinthians 1:20.

Going through this journey of healing I had support from my former pastor his wife and my husband. I needed that support from them too. My former mentor played a huge role in my journey to recovery. When therapy was hard, she would sit with me, talk to me, hug me, encourage me, cry with me and laugh with me. I didn't know what I would do without her in my life. During the 6th week of therapy, things got so bad; I spent three days back to back of being rushed to the hospital. My breathing and anxiety was at an all-time high. It felt like my world was caving in but God was carrying me afloat. He never let me sink. During this part of my journey in life, I was still ministering, helping the youth and others. I couldn't understand how God could use me so powerfully when I was going through healing, but he did. He used me in a mighty way. I still stayed before God and kept crying out to Him. When I would see other saints broken and messed up, it grieved my heart. I would weep before God for them. Some were so messed up they didn't even see they needed help. They were in a place of error and deeply wounded. I found myself crying out to God for them because although I was going through, I had surrendered myself unto God. One thing I know about this whole journey of my life even in a broken place in your life, you must have a submitted heart unto God and be honest with him about where you are in life. I was completely uncovered before God. I had nothing hidden and I cried out for His help during every aching moment of the process. I was not giving up and I was not going out without a fight and you will not give up either or stop fighting. You must remain steadfast on this journey and keep your eyes on Christ.

I'm not saying it's easy, but I found it a whole lot easier to keep focused on the Lord during this journey than to focus on what I was going through and the horrible memories of it. The fact of the matter is I'll never forget those horrific days. I remember them like yesterday but, the memories are no longer agonizing for me. I put my trust in confidence in God and not on my situation. I knew He is going to bring me out and you too. I am currently writing as I go through this journey and I must say today was tough. There will be moments when the enemy will bombard your thoughts with painful memories of those horrific days. Today was one of the days for me. I couldn't erase the images from my head of the torment I went through and I endured for years. The sexual abuse was hideous and no child should have to endure that at all, however, I did. My cousins took my ability to make a decision on my own. She repeatedly sexually molested me and took all my clothes off, sometimes during the day and no one ever noticed a thing. I learned sexual acts at four years old, I really learned them more at the age six and seven years old. What I endured was a tragedy that God was turning into triumph. It's wasn't easy going through the healing process. It's was tough at times, but I kept pressing and I kept fighting and I was determined to come out on top. I refuse to be robbed of the abundance of life that God intended for me. I won't let the enemy take another moment from me. Even when my days seem gloomy and overwhelming, I prayed. I would go into my prayer closet and I cry out to God. I layed it all before Him. Some nights I had to get prayer because the thought and memories of those days ripped through my head over and over again. I had to constantly read the word of God, play the word and speak the word over my life. When I say the word of God is powerful and works wonders, it really does. You just have to trust God at is His word. I was not giving up or turning back. I'm going keep rising in God and be that virtuous woman He called me to be. I say to you who are reading this don't give up even when it gets hard or when days seem tough. Revert to the word of God, incline yourself unto to God and continuously cry out before God because, He is who and what you need. He is the only one that can give you peace in the midst of the storm and in the midst of the journey. I am believing God for you right now that you are going to get through this. I believe every promise that God has made for you, you must believe as well. Believe that God is a healer, believe that he is a deliverer.

Dealing with my past, I am learning a lot about me and God is truly cleaning out all the ugly on the inside of me. I am learning that on this walk you have to be cleansed daily from the inside out. David said in Psalms, "Lord create in me a clean heart and renew the right spirit within me." This must be our daily prayer along with submitting to God and His will for our lives.

We have to allow God to be our leader in every decision of our lives. It's not about me anyway and I am really starting to get that. I also learned the power of love. When you can love even through your pain when it hurts yet you can still love, you know you are growing. God is doing something amazing on the inside of me and He is doing it for you too. Just trust His plan for your life and trust that He has our best interest at heart. God knows better than us. This is definitely a transformation process for me where God is transforming me from the inside out. The more I truly begin to depend on God and His plan for my life the greater the outcome is, I am an overcomer. When I depend upon God, I see things through His lens and not through the lens of the flesh. As a growing Prophet of I am learning that I don't know everything and a lot of times things and situations I am faced with in life and at church is not what it appears to be. Behind every tear, smile, and laugh there is a story, a story in people that I don't know. So I can never judge that which I think I know and see because only God knows the full story of what's really going on behind every smile, tear, and laugh. I know for me people always judged that which they thought they knew about me and of me they treated me according to that which they didn't even know. You see behind every smile was a bleeding heart. Behind every laugh was a cover up of shame and guilt that I felt inside. Behind every smile, I was crying for help. I had a feeling wanting to belong and fit in. My story was deep and I was in need of a lot of healing and deliverance. When because folk in church moved and acted on that which they thought they knew with me it crushed an already wounded soul. They didn't take the time to seek God concerning me and only saw through a natural lens, I was crucified on every mistake I made. Pushed deeper into a hole I was desperately trying to get out of. Through this experience, I learned not to judge that which I didn't know because I've been hurt, wounded and abused I could smell hurt a mile away. I knew what not to do, and I tried my best after being delivered not to do those things because I know what it felt like being done unto me. Even in my marriage, those around me ostracized me and magnified every issue I had. Yet my husband in other's eyes did no wrong. Everything was always me. Can you imagine? I'm already struggling with getting healed and delivered, yearning for God and didn't know how to go about forgiving? In the process of the pain, guilt and shame more of that was constantly being dumped on me. I tell you God had a mighty plan for my life. Though it didn't seem like it going through, I see the fruit and purpose behind everything I've been through. When God truly got a hold of my heart, He cleansed it, healed it and renewed it. What I loved and learned about this awesome God that we serve is that He will come and step right into your situation. He will meet you right where you are, when He steps into it great and mighty things happen. What people put their mouth on and said you couldn't do, God steps in and performs that thing right in you and through you. God will never give up on you. A lot of times we give up on ourselves and the amazing God we serve. I've learned and have seen far too often that we make our problems and situations bigger than God. He is way bigger than any problem or situation you may ever face in life.

I wasn't always at this place of trusting and believing God. The things I have been through and experienced in life brought me to a place of knowing that he is bigger than any situation or problem I may face. God is mighty and strong. I know He is bigger that my childhood, greater than the pain and definitely larger than my issues. I thank God for what He is doing in my life and for every obstacle he brought me through. I thank Him for every mountain He brought me over.

It has now been seven months into therapy and man has my life taking leaps and bounds. Depression no longer has a hold on my life. Shame, guilt, and dirtiness no longer have a grip on me. In fact, I am liberated in my mind and free in my emotions. My emotions have stabilized so much they are not all out of control. I don't become an emotional wreck when things don't go as I plan or something happens or said to me. God is doing an amazing thing inside of me and it's starting to show from the inside out. I don't have to pretend to be happy and full of life, I don't have to go around wearing a mask. I thank God for cleaning me up, looking beyond my faults and seeing the need. He never left me alone even in my darkest moment. He was there with me. When some gave up on me and spoke against me, God was there carrying me through. While I was going through the emotional healing, I took two months off of ministry for self-care. It was so hard for me, but I had to do what was best for me at that time. If you have ever been through emotional flooding, you will understand why I needed to take a step back from doing so much in church. The church could already be taxing and sometimes overwhelming with being over so many ministries. I didn't need anything taking away my energy while I went through emotional healing. I can say it was definitely worth it. But it took a lot of courage and strength. I had to keep my mind and eyes centered on God. I couldn't focus or center it on what others would think or say. I knew what I had to do and my mind was made up to go through this and come out made whole. For two months, I did not work the altar, preach, teach or mc. The only thing I continued to do was praise dance because it was also an outlet for me. It was the only place where I found myself forgetting about all of my issues and getting lost in praise and worship unto God. I was so free and felt so liberated whenever I would praise dance unto God.

Chapter Nine

Breakthrough At The Door

At the beginning of sitting down from the ministry, I was facing my fears, my past and the anxiety head on. I was at the end of this journey and many of you reading this know that when the enemy sees you at your breakthrough, he tries to come in like a flood. That's exactly what happened to me. I was in a vulnerable place and things were crashing all around me. It was a very difficult place where even my mentors and I didn't see eye to eye. Through all of that, I kept pressing no matter what anyone said about me or to me because my mind was made up to be made whole. One thing I love about this amazing God that I serve is that He would always send someone to encourage me. They would show up right at the moment I needed Him the most. I got up from that place and kept on fighting tooth and nail to come out. I would not give in to the pressure of giving up or giving in. God was bringing me out and it was about to manifest in a very great and powerful way. God was not leaving one stone in my life unturned.

Layer by layer things were coming off me and the more it did, the more liberated I felt on the inside. My focus and mindset was shifting. I was not tormented anymore.

From The Hospital To The Pulpit

My thoughts were clear and I was beginning to see light at the end of the tunnel. When you want something so bad you go after it with everything within you and you let nothing stand in your way. That's how I was about being made whole and coming out of what I was in. I no longer desired to stay stuck in my past, stuck in bitterness, jealousy, envy, strife or anger. Shame no longer had control over me and neither did guilt. I was beginning to see myself as God did and not what others thought of me. My confidence was growing and the more I got into the word of God the more it took root and transformed my life. I even began to feel a difference in my health. I went from going to the hospital almost every month to none at all. The spiritual surgery that God was performing on my heart was real and true and it was evident in my life. I no longer had to pretend. I was healed or changed because it was actually showing in my life. People saw the difference including my family and it had a huge impact on their lives. I was no longer that angry, bitter Ronisha, but now I was full of love and life-giving love and also receiving it. What a blessing to be able to first receive the love God has for you and to be able to give it in return.

This was the place I was looking forward to and where God had taken me to. It took work determination and consistency with letting God move and have His way with my life. God has even restored a very valuable relationship in my life with a very good friend of me since 2005. When we first met, we bonded so well it was amazing, but of course that was during the time I had my issues and suffered from rejection. When we got too close, I would push her away or just shut completely down. She would always come and talk to me even though things were rough in our friendship. At the time I couldn't see my own faults or issues, so I blamed others instead of taking ownership of my actions. There were things that hurt me as well that I never spoke about but would have to let it all go for the greater in God. One thing I encourage you to do is take ownership of your actions, problems, and situations. I find that things go a lot smoother when we are honest with ourselves and allow God in. I also believe that to first have healthy relationships with people we must first have a healthy relationship with God. One thing that I know about this great and mighty God that I serve is that there is nothing lacking in Him. The key word in Him: Being connected to Him is the source of power. God in His awesomeness knows how to work all things out for our good. He was restoring things and relationships in my life and I was forever grateful.

God was shifting things inside of me. He was repositioning me in Him and He was sure opening my eyes to a lot in Him. One thing I love about this journey is how God cleans you on the inside and there is no pretense or falseness. He brings you from that place and state of being to a place of origination.
When you're clean on the inside it shows on the outside. This joy and love that you have, the world did not give it and neither can the world take it away. My joy is not founded in things, money, relationships, but in God. I have true joy now, and I am not ashamed of where God has brought me from. It was the making of Ronisha. I am so grateful I did not abort the journey. I

did not give up because this breakthrough that I received is awesome. Layers of pain are gone and I am no longer a survivor, but I am Victorious. I have overcome. All these years, I learned how to survive in my mess, survive in depression, survive in rejection, abandonment, molestation and fear. God moved me from that place of surviving to overcoming it all and walking in victory. I give God all the praise, glory and honor for all He is doing and going to do. What are you? Where are you? Are you just surviving or are you overcoming? There is a huge difference, you see the pain no longer has power over me.
Rejection, bitterness, anger, resentment all those things no longer have power over me. I can talk about what I went through and share my story. It doesn't cause me to be an emotional wreck. I now have overcome those things and I put everything in its proper place.

God has delivered me from it all and I have overcome. I am no longer a survivor but an overcomer. You that are reading this and struggling at this very present moment, some of you crying as you're reading God is shifting you from being a survivor to overcoming. This thing will no longer have power over you, your emotions or your circumstances. As you go through your journey of healing and deliverance, remember that God is bringing you from surviving this thing to total victory. You're an overcomer. The word of God says we are overcome by the blood of the lamb and the words of our testimony. Keep pushing and keep pressing. There is more God has for you again there is nothing lacking including the need for emotional healing. I'm a living witness to the power of God in my life. The power of His unchanging word brought life and healing in areas I never thought I would experience. I also would like to clarify a few things concerning healing and deliverance. I do believe the church has been in error when it comes to deliverance and healing. This is what I have experienced in the body of Christ and what God has revealed to me on this journey. It is in error. For years in church, I was also told that I was the hindrance in my marriage and I was hindering my husband's walk with the Lord. I would get prayer. People would stand over me each in my ear yelling and telling me to let it go and they would bind this and that. One would stand there and say cough it up and here I would cough because I wanted to be whole so badly. If nothing came up, I would make it come up so they would stop hounding me and yelling in my ear. I call it my good ear (smile) but let's stay focused on the matter at hand. I would spend hours getting prayer and let me just say when I got up off that floor, I felt horrible.

My stomach would be in knots and sore the next day and barely could move I still felt bad or even worse after the prayers. It was a feeling of guilt that overwhelmed me. I could remember crying on my bed saying God am I that bad? I felt so unworthy, unwanted like a ball of shame. I went through this for years and no change not because I did not want it either because I did. I always yearned for God and wanted to be whole in Him but at that price, no. In the eyes of most around me and I say, most, because no one at that time in my life could see past the shell of my being. My former mentor did she was amazing. That's what I was judged on, my shell. God in His grace and mercy would always send someone I didn't know to speak a word of hope and encouragement in the midst of chaos. So, let me just say the moment I began to experience true healing and deliverance in Christ was when I truly began to work the word of God and allowed it according to Hebrews 4:12 to penetrate every core of my being. It cut and pierced me in every way. It's not your job to cut the word will do that all by it well with much conviction. I had to apply the word of God in every area of my life. I had to yield to the word of God. When I say the word cuts deep, it does, but it's also quickens which means it make you live. If we allow it to come alive in us, it will destroy every ungodly thing and uproot the root of bitterness and rejection all of it. The word of God is so powerful it will quicken you and you will begin to live. Don't get me wrong now sometimes it takes deliverance where there is coughing up even spirits that will manifest by screaming, coughing and things like that. However even in that when it's all done you must still maintain that place of healing and deliverance by living according to the word. I'll put it to you like this Romans 12:1 says, "I beseech you, therefore, brethren, by the mercies of God, that ye present your bodies a living sacrifice, holy, acceptable unto God, which is your reasonable service." So in other words, after you get done sobbing, speaking in tongues and crying out at the altar you must still get up and present. Be present wherever God is. Presenting will cause you to be in a place where His presence is and because of that holiness will take place. Holiness is acceptable to God there for it is your reasonable service.

From The Hospital To The Pulpit

We must present whatever is acceptable to God not to man. If what you are presenting is not acceptable to God it will not be a reasonable service. We must maintain that place of healing and deliverance rather your deliverance was coughing up, screaming, crying. The word of God must still take root in our lives and we must work the word of God, and that requires discipline. I learned this after all the dreadful coughing and torture I went through. In my case, I didn't need all that I just simply needed to let the word of God transform my life. Every story is different and every case is different. So as the Lord leads you on this journey through healing and deliverance just remember you still must live the word and allow it to transform your life. You must obey the word and what it says. It will save you from an emotional roller coaster. Now also never force deliverance. If you're not ready to give up something or let it go then be honest and ask God to give you the desire to be made whole. One reason why is because demons and spirits are not attracted to the world or people they already influence. They are attracted to clean temples. Read Mathew 12:44-45 "Then he saith, I will return into my house from whence I came out; and when he is come, he findeth it empty, swept, and garnished. Then goeth he, and taketh with himself seven other spirits more wicked than himself, and they enter in and dwell there: and the last state of that man is worse than the first. Even so shall it be also unto this wicked generation." When the place is empty of the demonic oppression you must fill that void now with the word of God. You can't leave it void and empty. This requires word on your part.

I am at a place now where it's all of God or nothing, giving Him half just won't work. There is such an inner peace I have I can't explain it. God did this for me. It's like once you cross over, your appetite for God increases, your eyes are open, and you see things clearly. There's such an overwhelming joy that fills your soul. I never in a million years would have thought I would be at a place of such freedom and liberty. The very word God spoke over me when I was messed up was delayed but not denied. He was going to give me an accelerated anointing. He has done just that and more. I have only been preaching since April 18th, 2015 and God has truly shifted me in ways I never would have imagined.

You may be at a place where people doubt you and they cast you off saying all manner of evil about you. Let them talk, let them doubt, but let God do the work in you and bring you into full being in Him. I know it hurts and your saying Lord I am trying. But, get the word of God with everything within you and pray the word over your life. This is the fight of your life, but God is with you. This journey takes work. My healing and deliverance didn't come overnight. I had made up in my mind that I was going with God all the way no matter the oppositions that came. I had a I won't give up in my spirit. I kept pressing no matter what it looked like. I kept my eyes on God because He was the only one that could bring me out of it. I had to declare the word of God and not only that believe it but have a sure

confidence in the word. Don't waver. Your flesh is not going to want to go. It's going to fight. That's why it's imperative that you yield your body unto fruits of righteousness. Romans 6:16 says "Know ye not, that to whom ye yield yourselves servants to obey, his servants ye are to whom ye obey; whether of sin unto death, or of obedience unto righteousness?" Yield yourself unto God and fruits of righteousness that you may obey the spirit of God and his word. You will be enslaved to whatever you yield your member to your body including your mind. So many of you will be found
reading this and at this place, a shift will take place freedom is at your door. There is nothing like the freedom of the Lord. I decree and declare that you are being set free right now. God is giving you tenacity to stand and press through. You're coming out of
this thing and it will no longer keep you in bondage. It will no longer keep you captive. Freedom is what the Lord says. Now get up from where you are and fight back, cry out to God and then get up and work the word of God.

"Now there was a long war between the house of Saul and the house of David: but David waxed stronger and stronger, and the house of Saul waxed weaker and weaker."

 Long war we sometimes don't like the term and want all storms, test, and trials to end quickly. However, God did not design things to go that way. When spirits gain a stronghold in our lives, it never happens overnight, but we want them gone fast. The root of a matter took time to sink and become a stronghold. So we must go through sometimes a long war for them being loosed from our lives. If you're praying against a stubborn stronghold in your life, you have to know it's not going out without a fight. If you keep putting pressure on the enemy, it will eventually become weaker and weaker and you will become stronger and stronger. Spirits cannot handle long war so when they try and hold on you have to keep praying, crying out to God, declaring the word of God over your life and pleading the blood of Jesus. It will get weaker and weaker and lose you. They can't stay where the word of God is constantly being fed because the word of God is quick, living and it will destroy every dead thing in you that's not right.

Long war does not mean you're losing the battle either. I was struggling with depression and rejection for years. It was rooted in me, so it wasn't easy to come out. It was like the weeds in the garden that you have to cut and pull on it several times before it comes out. I had to pray but not just prayer alone. I had to read the word and live what I was reading. It weakened the spirit and I became stronger over time. It then loosed its hold and I was set free. But through that long war, I learned how to war. I learned how to stand, trust and believe God at His word. I learned to use the power I possessed on the inside of me when God put His spirit in me.
Through the long war, the Lord will teach you how to war, how to use your weapons of warfare because they are not carnal but mighty through God to the pulling down of strongholds. The greatest warriors in the kingdom of God are those who have endured every battle to the end and came out victorious. God is no

respecter of persons and what He did for me He will do for you.

So no matter what it looks like with the natural eye, through faith you have to see yourself coming out. You have to see yourself victorious over it. You have to weaken every stronghold as you become stronger until it loses it hold on you.

For you all that are reading and have given up because what you were hoping for seemed differed or overlooked. Keep reading.

Proverbs 13:12

"Hope deferred maketh the heart sick: but when the desire cometh, it is a tree of life."

Three key components in coming out and being made free, the word of God accompanied with prayer and fasting. Don't ever just seek to get head knowledge of scripture we must always live what we speak concerning the word of God, obey the word. Praying the word of God is a key and one of the most powerful things to do. It will enhance your prayer life and give revelatory insight on the word of God. It enlarges your ability and capacity to pray and pull-down strongholds. It will bring you into a place of knowing the will of God. The will of God is the word of God and the Bible tells us not to be unwise concerning the will of God. Ephesians 5:17 "Wherefore be ye not unwise, but understanding what the will of the Lord is."

I am doing the will of God as I write the ending of this book. I am doing what God spoke over my life even before I was born. I came from the hospital bed to the pulpit and it's evident in my life that God's hand is on it. Deliverance breaks forth every time God opens the door for me to speak. So many lives are changed and set free and it makes me even more grateful that I endured everything I went through. I am seeing the fruit of my transformed life everything is falling into to place. I just launched my website rorishawilliams.com. Subscribe so you can be updated when I'm speaking, or my next book is out. I am so excited the feeling I have on the inside is unexplainable and you know what no one can take away what God has done for me. I'm no longer on an emotional rollercoaster.

I have stability in my life. My mind is stable and no longer double-minded, but every area in my life is stable. You know what else is so awesome? Because of this freedom and liberty in Christ, even my health has taken a 360 turn around for the good. My marriage is great and my relationship with my kids is good. I know who I am in God and I'm walking in the calling, anointing, and authority He has placed over my life. You know what else is so amazing? God is about to do this for you too. And you will go and share and others will be set free too. From the hospital bed to the pulpit God is using me like never before, and I say all glory belongs to God. I can't give credit to no man because God is the only one who brought me out.

Jeremiah 29:11

From The Hospital To The Pulpit

"For I know the thoughts that I think toward you, saith the Lord, thoughts of peace, and not of evil, to give you an expected end."

Speak them over your life and have a sure confidence of what the word is saying and don't doubt. This requires work on your part to do daily along with prayer and fasting. The enemy will not go out without a fight but be confident God has equipped you with everything you need. Many are being made free now. You've got tenacity and you're ready. You must also have a made-up mind that no matter the opposition you coming out. Get all the scriptures concerning the liberty, freedom, healing, love and declare the word of God over your life. They stronghold will weaken and you will become stronger and finally it will lose its hold on you.

Don't give up and keep pressing. You're a jewel. The Bible says you're fearfully and wonderfully made. God is with you, and because He is for you, He is more than the whole world against you. I love you but God loves you more, and God wants you free indeed.

I now reside in Dallas, TX and God has continuously showed himself mighty and strong. Weeks into my journey of healing I knew I would transition soon. I appreciate every moment I had and what I learned and experience with my former leaders. No one can take what they've been to me. I will forever love and cherish them.

I am called to be God's prophet and His mouthpiece to the nations. It's important that you're also at the right place for you to grow. A religious institution will not do it. I stayed bound for so many years because of that as well. Look to the Lord. He heard my cries and he hears yours. That is why you have to keep fighting and keep pushing no matter what you're faced with. Hold on to God with all that's within you. God is shifting things even now for you. Trust in the Lord with all thine heart and never lean to your own understanding. If your leaning on your friends that's not trusting God. You're leaning on your understanding. We must always lean on God and His understanding. I decree and declare every reader is shifting in your mind heart and spirit. You will never be the same and God sees you.

Note: My prayer is that every reader be transformed by the power of God. Deal with every WHY in your life and stop hiding. Deal with the why behind your dysfunctional, hurt, anger, addiction, resentment, deceit and messiness. Deal with why you struggle with trusting and needing a man/woman. Deal with why you feel lonely.

I encourage you to give it all you got. The destiny that's on the inside of you, it's bigger than you. The Why in your life is hidden hinderances. That's why you can only go so far before you're faced with your WHY. I had to face every Why in my life. It brought me to a place of total VICTORY. I have freedom in being who God has created me to be with no secrets. Stop holding back your destiny awaits you.

From The Hospital To The Pulpit

This is a critical hour we are in and the enemy knows his time is almost up. Don't waste another moment being stuck, being bound. God has great need of you in the kingdom of God there is room for you here.

To every leader; ministry is quite costly don't you agree? It's imperative we don't lead while bleeding that we make sure we are whole. It's okay to take time as a leader and heal. Love you enough to heal.

You have to touch the Holy Ghost in this hour, touch means to cling unto. You have to touch the Holy Ghost until your change comes. Touch the Holy Ghost until He becomes your manifested reality. Touch him until your breakthrough, touch Him until your family is changed. You have to cling on until virtue from Jesus comes upon you.

You have to wait until He comes in and stay until He finishes with you. Your on a path that will shift your life to Jesus being your complete reality.

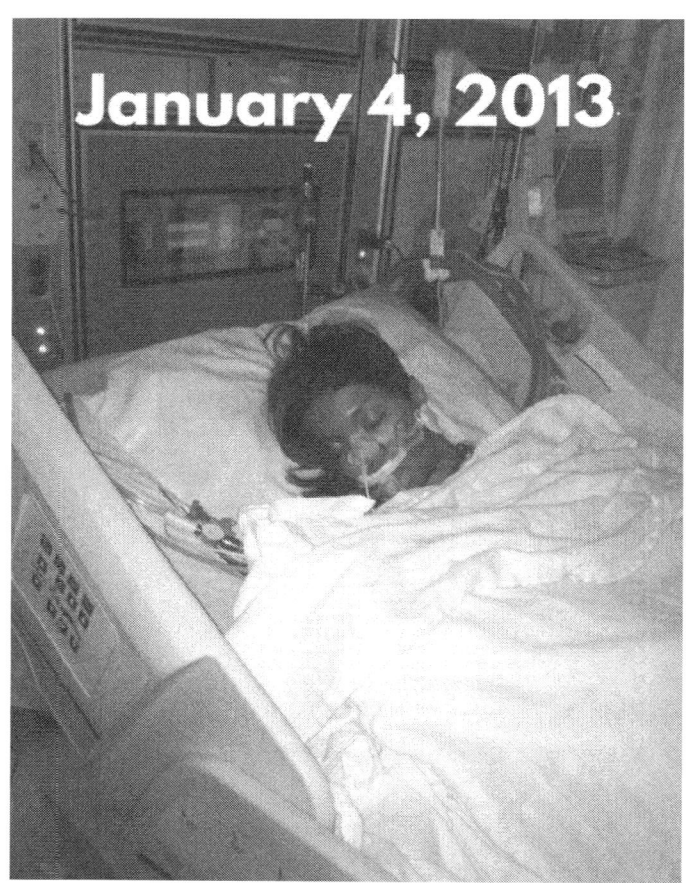

From The Hospital To The Pulpit

From The Hospital To The Pulpit

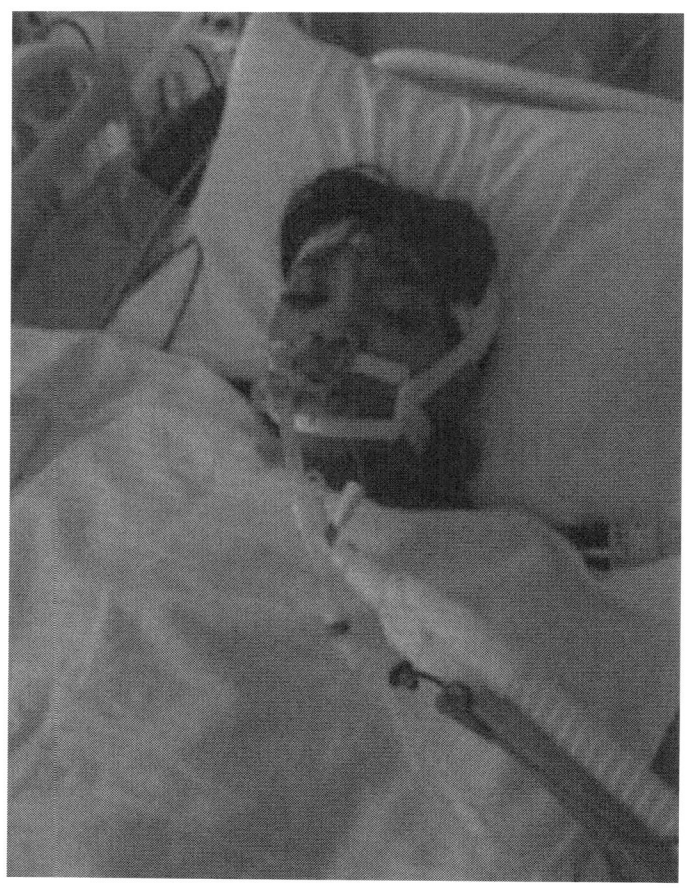

From The Hospital To The Pulpit

Made in the USA
Middletown, DE
02 July 2020